Volume 2

understanding
human behavior

An Illustrated Guide to Successful Human Relationships

COLUMBIA HOUSE / New York

Editor	Nicolas Wright
Deputy Editor	Susan Joiner
Senior Designer	Stewart Cowley
Art Editor	Mary Cooper
Art Assistant	Jeff Gurney
Editorial Assistants	Mundy Ellis
	Sarie Forster
	John Moore
	Michael McIntyre
Picture Research	Diane Rich
	Hazel Robinson
	Paul Snelgrove
Editorial Director	Graham Donaldson

Production Manager: Warren E. Bright
Cover Design: Harry W. Fass
Cover Photo: Jon Silla

ACE of WANDS.   ACE of CUPS.   ACE of SWORDS.   ACE of PENTACLES.

THE HIGH PRIESTESS.   THE EMPRESS.   THE EMPEROR.   THE HIEROPHANT.

WHEEL of FORTUNE.   JUSTICE.   THE HANGED MAN.   DEATH.

contents

introduction

There can be no doubt that a great many married women are becoming increasingly dissatisfied with their role and status. They would, it seems, far rather work in an office than stay at home. And they would prefer working in a factory to cleaning the house.

Why is it they feel this way? Is it a long overdue reaction to social conditioning and the traditional assumption that the woman's place is in the home, looking after her husband and bringing up children? In this, the second volume of *Understanding Human Behavior,* we examine the married woman's role and outline at least some of the reasons why that role is now being so heavily questioned.

As well as explaining why we think and act how we do, *Understanding Human Behavior* will, throughout the series, be taking a comprehensive and detailed look at the way in which our body actually works. For instance, did you know that we are controlled by a complex system of internal clocks? These determine when we go to sleep, when we wake up or when we feel hungry. They regulate our levels of efficiency and have altogether a far greater impact on our lives than most people realize.

If you have a job then you also have a boss. But what kind of person is he? They are all different. Some are timid, others brash, some thoughtful, others aggressive and dictatorial. Whatever pattern your boss fits there's a reason for it. And by understanding that reason you could make your own life a lot easier.

(continued)

In our firm belief that *Understanding Human Behavior* should not shy away from the real facts of life, Volume Two contains the first two parts of a far-reaching discussion on sex. All your questions are answered: What exactly is a "normal" sex life? What is sexual perversion? Can we do without sex altogether? What is homosexuality? You will find the answers as frank and honest as the questions!

Each article in this volume and all the successive volumes will provide some fresh insight into the way we behave and the factors governing that behavior. Jealousy, for instance; the things which can go wrong on honeymoon; what makes us superstitious or why so many of us believe in the supernatural.

Find out more about your inner self and discover what makes you behave the way you do.

—The Editor

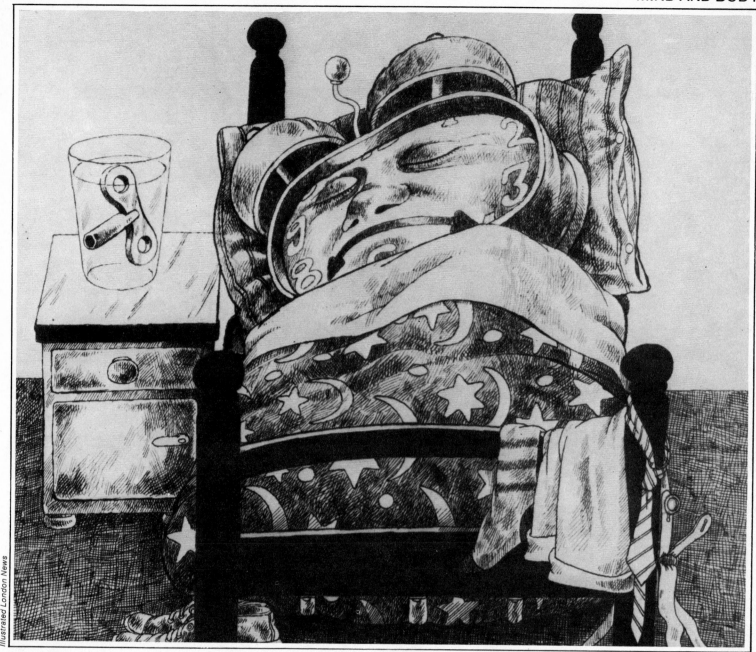

Illustrated London News

How you tick

Are you an "Owl" or a "Lark"? Do you find it difficult to get up in the morning or are you at your best before 9:00 a.m.? Our bodily rhythms are controlled by a number of internal biological clocks which, if understood, can make our lives a lot easier and happier.

Michel Siffre, a young French geologist, once spent 63 days in a cave deep under the Alps. And although his sleeping and waking patterns maintained their normal 24-hour rhythm, he eventually emerged thinking he had been there only 36 days.

Our bodies, as Siffre's experience showed, have an accurate sense of time, even when our actual judgment of time lets us down. You can prove this to yourself by a simple test. When you go to bed, make up your mind to wake up at seven or at seven-thirty. You will find it quite easy to do. In fact most of us, unless we are particularly tired, wake up just before the alarm clock goes off.

Death Comes in the Morning

If you are still alive at ten in the morning, you will probably live another day, no matter how ill you are. Most people die in the early morning.

Our energy, or the strength of the chemical process that keeps us alive, drops in the early morning, irrespective of whether we are asleep or awake. And if you want to be there when your wife has a baby, prepare to be up early. Most normal births happen between midnight and eight in the morning.

There seem to be a number of clocks working inside us, and if we understand them, we can make our

Michel Siffre, a French geologist, spent 63 days in a subterranean cave. Although he thought that he had been down there for only 36 days, his body rhythms kept an exact schedule throughout his long stay.

is lunch time in London when you arrive. But to your body, it is six o'clock in the evening, and in about four hours, it will start to shut down. You will get sleepy at six o'clock by British time.

There is nothing very surprising in this, because you got up at your normal time in America. But what is unexpected is that the same pattern will continue no matter what you do, for three or four days. So, if you have important decisions to make, make them in the morning. Your mind will be as wide-awake as it would be in the afternoon in the country you left behind, whereas if you wait until the afternoon, your body will be closing down for the night. Those who are involved in meetings that last all day should arrive three or four days before the meetings start. Russian diplomats always do.

Getting Used to Shift Work

The jet set are not the only sufferers from the stability of their internal clocks. About a fifth of the workers in the industrialized countries work in shifts, and someone whose working day starts at a normal time will have to work at night later on in the year. Again, the change takes the body by surprise, and the worker will be less efficient, less healthy and less happy until he has reset his internal clock. For the good of the worker as well as the factory, shifts should be changed as infrequently as possible.

If the internal clock is allowed to settle down, then the worker becomes accustomed to his unusual day, and at least one study has shown that night workers are actually healthier than those on the day shift, although this may be partly because they have a much easier journey to and from their work. Those who can never let their clocks reset—long distance jet pilots, for example, are less healthy and have shorter lives than the average, and this is not simply a matter of the strain of flying airliners in crowded airways. Pilots on internal flights or flights within a single time zone have a normal expectation of life.

The daily rhythm—the circadian rhythm as scientists call it—is the most important one. But there are quicker rhythms. Twice a day, at

lives easier and happier, healthier and even more successful.

A knowledge of the fundamental rhythms to which our bodies are attuned is now recognized as being of practical importance in physiology and medicine, in industry, in transport, in the regulation of exercise, rest and diet, and even perhaps in space flight. These bodily rhythms range over at least a dozen frequencies. At one extreme there is the repeated firing of an impulse in a nerve fiber. At the other, there is the complete life cycle from conception to death.

The most obvious rhythm is the daily one. Every night, our processes shut down. Our brain switches off the part that arouses attention, our heart rate slows. This is very stable.

Plan an Early Arrival

It is this daily rhythm that causes what we now call "jet lag," although the problem affects anyone who travels quickly from one time zone to another. If you travel from America to Britain you arrive at much the same time, by the sun, as you took off. If you leave New York at lunch time, it

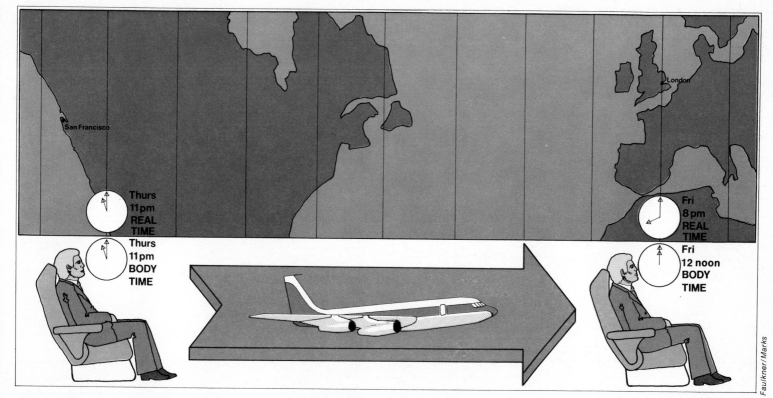

Faulkner/Marks

The marvels of modern technology enable man to cross the Atlantic in less than six hours. But is it worth it? After a long flight politicians and businessmen must rest before making any important decisions. This is to allow their biological time clocks to adjust. Pilots who also suffer from the condition known as "jet lag" are not so fortunate. Statistics show that their life expectation is shortened by their work. The picture above shows how we are thrown out of gear by a transatlantic flight. Research into man's biological time mechanism has revealed two rhythms at work (right). The first (in red) is the active energy level, which reaches a high point in most people at 9 a.m. and 6 p.m. with a low period at 3 a.m. The second rhythm (in blue) is cell regeneration, which works in reverse with a low point at 9 a.m. and a high at 12 midnight.

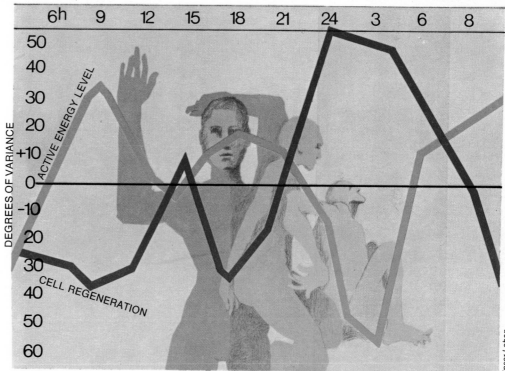

Unser Leben

about 1:00 p.m. and 9:00 p.m., the heart muscle rate slows, pumping less blood, and while we expect to be below our best in the late evening, not everyone knows that his efficiency also falls towards lunch time. Where we can make a check, the results confirm that we are more careful, more alert, and more able between 8:00 a.m. and noon and between 2:00 and 5:00 p.m.

Factory workers make more mistakes towards the end of these periods than at the beginning, and it has nothing to do with the time they have

spent working or the time between meals. The conventional lunch time, though, is a good way of keeping workers away from their benches during their least effective periods.

Lark and Owl Temperaments

The peaks of ability seem to apply to everyone, but within them there are individual differences that we can profit by recognizing. Some people seem to have the "lark" temperament, others the "owl." "Larks" find it easy to get up in the morning and are at their best before lunch. After

lunch they are well below it. Others, the owls, have barely woken by the time they start their day's work, and are at their best after lunch.

These differences are outside our control—it is not merely a matter of will power. An "owl's" heart rate will not be normal until an hour or two after waking up, and his temperature will be slightly subnormal, and for the same time all his bodily processes will still be recovering from their nighttime shutdown. It seems as if the differences between "larks" and "owls" are inherited, so you might as

Bob Estall

Mark Edwards

Spectrum

Faulkner/Marks

Experiments have shown that it is possible to establish body clocks on many levels, with cycles varying from minutes to years. Here, in the classic response-reward situation, a cat was given food after pressing a bar, but *only* at eight-minute intervals, no matter how often it touched the bar between those times. After some early random tries, the cat soon learned to press the bar almost exactly after eight minutes had elapsed, as the graph above shows. In humans as well, this kind of habitual expectation tells us when we are hungry and when it is time to eat. It is also the reason most sleepers waken just before the alarm clock goes off or commuters look up from their books just before the right train stop. Conditioning programs this anticipation into our behavior, and it soon becomes an automatic response.

Until the industrial revolution man rose and went to bed with the sun. Today biological clocks are often altered to fit the demands of modern life. Many people work shifts which do not correspond with daylight hours, but in time they adapt quite successfully.

well decide which one you are and plan your day to fit your changing efficiency. You will not be able to change your temperament.

Anyone who is planning a team project can choose whether to mix larks and owls, so that part of the team is at its best while the other part is not, or to have a team composed only of either larks or owls, so that everyone is at their best during the same period. The American Space Agency, as it happens, never mixes larks and owls. On the other hand, if the popular belief is true, owls nearly always marry larks.

Our lives are also marked by rhythms that beat less than once a day. We know we have "good" and "bad" days, but may not suspect that they are the result of our biology. Individual patients in mental hospitals can have regular cycles in which they change from being apparently normal to being clearly disturbed, and any doctor who has to decide if a patient will be able to fit into the world outside must be sure he is investigating him on a "bad" day. On the other hand, we should do our business on our good days, and there is on record an insurance salesman who discovered that he was markedly depressed every other day. He simply struck these days from his diary, and worked on alternate days.

In spite of the meticulous regularities of our body rhythms, there is a curious discrepancy which becomes increasingly disconcerting as the years pass by. Most people sadly remark that, as they grow older, the years seem to flash by with ever growing speed; in other words, there is an apparent acceleration in the flow of calendar time. This is known as "Janet's law," after the French psychiatrist who first formulated it. We can express it another way by saying that with advancing age our biological clocks slow down relative to the constant speed of calendar time.

Medical scientists, in recent decades, have been actively investigating the bearing of bodily rhythms on different diseases. Some 40 years ago Swedish doctors established that, when treating diabetics with insulin, the hour of the day when the insulin is administered ought to be taken into account, because of variation in the blood sugar at different times in the 24-hour period. Following this discovery, cyclic features in the symptoms of other ailments were identified and related to diurnal rhythms in the composition of the blood, in the gastric juices and in excreta.

A Drug at the Right Time

Such fluctuations are now recognized as important in the treatment of blood, heart and glandular diseases. Thus, blood pressure, following a circadian rhythm, is lowest in the morning and highest in the evening, so a drug for low blood pressure should be taken in the morning; and one for high blood pressure in the evening.

Articular dropsy or hydrarthrosis, a condition in which the joints swell as a result of fluid flowing into the cavities, aptly illustrates a rhythm which varies from limb to limb and from patient to patient, though the cycle is constant in any given individual.

In one patient, a 47-year-old man, there were signs of two clocks, each marking a cycle of about 7 days. One was associated with a swelling of the right knee, and the other with a swelling of the left knee. Often the swelling in the one was greatest when it was least in the other. The right knee of another patient swelled on Tuesdays and Wednesdays, and the left knee on Thursdays and Fridays. A star footballer, who was a victim of the same

Modern scientists are not the first to see man's body as a clock.

disease, found that his knee joints would swell regularly every nine days. Matches were arranged to suit his rhythms.

From the rhythms our bodies keep in health, and the way they are disturbed when we are ill, we can draw guidance as to what and when we should eat and as to when we should exert ourselves, relax or sleep. Heavy physical effort is to be shunned when our blood sugar is low lest excessive strain should affect the muscles of the heart. Protein and fatty foods should be taken earlier in the day, carbohydrates later. It is not conducive to health to overload the stomach with heavy meat or fat in the evening; and to ensure a good night's sleep, alcohol should be consumed in moderation before retiring for the night.

Learning from Insects

Light may be thrown on the course of human disease by the study of biological clocks of other species. A remarkable illustration is the success of Dr. Janet Harker, at Cambridge, in locating a 24-hour clock in the neurosecretory cells of the cockroach. This insect is quiescent by day and active by night. Its biological clock announces the onset of dark. Under conditions of continuous light or continuous dark the cycle tends to disappear; the cockroach is then active around the clock with intermittent rest intervals.

Dr. Harker kept one group of cockroaches in artificial light during the night and in the dark during daytime, until their inner clocks were reset to beat 12 hours out of phase with

other cockroaches: they were active in the *true* day and quiescent in the *true* night. She then implanted the neurosecretory cells of these out-of-phase creatures into normal insects. The latter now had two contradictory clocks, one telling them, as it were, that it was dark and to move about; the other telling them that it was light and they should be immobile. Nearly all developed malignant tumors of the intestine as a result of this "nervous" strain.

Further studies of the internal clocks of other creatures show that birds wake or sleep according to the daylight. The "dawnchorus" happens more or less at dawn, and all the birds of an area go to sleep during an eclipse of the sun. But migrant birds and racing pigeons use internal clocks of astonishing accuracy, combined with their observation of the sun's position, to know exactly where they are.

One aspect of human inner clocks seems like science fiction and yet may be perfectly real. According to Einstein's Theory of Relativity, time can contract or expand according to the speed of bodies in space in relation to those fixed on earth. One consequence of this could affect astronauts who, on journeys to the moon, may return a fraction of a second younger than those they left behind on earth.

Journey Through Time

There could be a far-reaching effect on an astronaut, traveling close to the speed of light, i.e. 186,000 miles a second, who undertakes longer voyages which last several decades. If, according to the theory, earth time under these conditions passes five times as fast as spacecraft time, after 50 earth years only 10 years would have elapsed on the spacecraft. The astronaut would then return a younger man than the son he left behind him.

It was the great French philosopher René Descartes who appears to have been the first to think of living things as governed by inner clocks. In 1646 he wrote to the Marquis of Newcastle, saying: "I know, indeed, that brutes do many things better than we do, but I am not surprised at it; for that, also, goes to prove that they act by force of nature and by springs, like a clock, which tells better what the hour is than our judgment can inform us. And doubtless when swallows come in the spring, they act in that like clocks. All that honey bees do is of the same nature; and the order that cranes keep in flying, or monkeys drawn up for battle . . ."

Keystone

Sex & Dominance

Among animals the dominant five percent always assume control but the rigid structure of human society often thwarts natural leaders. If men like Churchill, Roosevelt and Stalin are an uncommon breed, opportunities for their emergence are more rare still.

Who are the alphas, these dominant personalities? From which section of society do they come? Are the children of alphas always alphas too? The dominants arise in any and every section of society—always in the same proportions.

It does not make any difference which position in the social hierarchy was occupied by the individual's parents. If dominance could be inherited then soon the community would be a society comprising all chiefs and no Indians—a potentially dangerous state of affairs. The point

is that alphas are attractive to the other members of the group—they have the personal magnetism and the status to get what they want.

Stopping POWs from Escaping

It was Robert Ardrey, the American author of *African Genesis*, who first gave publicity to the "one in twenty" theory. Ardrey's research showed him that one of the most closely guarded secrets of the Korean War was that no escapes were made by American prisoners. This was because their Chinese captors had dis-

covered an infallible method of preventing breakouts. They observed the prisoners carefully for a while, then removed the "dominant" ones—the five percent who were leader figures—and put them in a separate compound under heavy guard. Once the leaders were removed, the other prisoners became far easier to handle—in fact, they could be left with almost no guard at all. The Chinese observed that the number of dominant prisoners was always exactly one in twenty.

The Nazis recognized the significance of this when, during World

War II, they placed all the most incorrigible escapers together in "escape-proof" prisons like Colditz. More recently, in Britain, the 1966 commission into prison reform headed by Lord Louis Mountbatten recommended that the more dangerous convicts were not split up among a large number of prisons, but were kept together.

Call for Study of Dominance

So far, however, no zoologist has conducted careful research to establish why the dominant minority appears to be five percent. A study should be made of leading surgeons, ministers, politicians, sportsmen, and pop stars to ascertain whether or not they form five percent of the population. Obviously it is not only criminals who are dominant; Ardrey defines dominance as occurring when "two or more animals (or humans) pursue the same activity."

The view is also held that crooks only become crooks because their will power is so frustrated or denied in some way—thus rechanneling their efforts to succeed into antisocial areas. One of the few countries where official figures are available is Russia, where the Communist Party of the Soviet Union contains approximately five percent of all the people—14½ million members out of a population of 242 million.

In the United States, scientific probes have been made into the whole question of dominance, and the researches of John B. Calhoun at the National Institute of Mental Health at Bethseda, Maryland threw up one of the most disturbing observations on the subject of power over others. Calhoun wanted to observe the behavior of rats under conditions of overcrowding to examine their responses.

A large number of rats were placed in three interconnecting cages. The "king rat" took over the central cage for himself and his harem; the other rats were forced into the other two cages, so they were now grossly overcrowded. And the dominant five percent quickly became a criminal five percent. These "criminal rats" did things that are never seen among rats in nature. Rats ordinarily have an elaborate and self-protecting courting ritual; but these overcrowded rodents wandered around in gangs, raping any spare females they chanced upon. They also became cannibals, eating the baby rats.

Among animal groups the alpha is given the go-ahead to have as much sex as he desires. Invariably he has

During World War II, the Germans imprisoned dominant POWs in Colditz, a top security prison. The number of escapes was thus drastically reduced. But what makes for dominance? Statistics show that of two eggs laid by the kittiwake, the first to hatch is dominant while among humans, eldest sons also tend to be the dominant offspring.

more sex than the other males and for the reasons mentioned the alpha not only has the pick of the females, he also tends to have more than one mate. Even among human beings this is true: the dominant male has first choice of the women and he is promiscuous. Incidentally the same principles apply to the dominant woman.

A young psychologist called Abraham Maslow spent hours watching monkeys in the Bronx Zoo, New York. Their behavior puzzled him. To begin with, they seemed to think of nothing but sex, said Maslow. But that was more or less explainable to a Freudian. After all, Freud had asserted that sex is the basic impulse in all animals. What baffled Maslow in this simian Sodom and Gomorrah was that male apes mounted other males, females mounted other females and on occasion, females even mounted males.

135

Were they all "wantons"? And then, one day, the answer struck him. It was always the highly dominant apes that mounted the less dominant ones, and it made no difference whether they were male or female. He was witnessing the ape's "pecking order."

This made Maslow interested in the whole phenomenon of dominance. Maybe Freud was wrong about the importance of sex. The logical thing, Maslow decided, was to study dominance in women—the naturally undominant sex. Between 1937 and the early '40s, he made careful case studies of nearly 200 women. The results, when he published them, were so startling that psychologists did not know what to make of them.

Three Kinds of Women

What was so remarkable was that the women seemed to fall quite clearly into *three* groups, which Maslow labeled High Dominance, Medium Dominance and Low Dominance. High dominance women tended to be highly sexed. Most of them masturbated without feeling guilt; they enjoyed sexual experimentation; they were promiscuous. Many had had lesbian experience. In order to achieve full sexual satisfaction, these women needed a highly dominant male. One highly dominant woman was a nymphomaniac who could have an orgasm just by looking at a man; yet with one male, she had been unable to achieve a climax because "I just couldn't respect him."

Medium dominance women tended to be gentle souls, altogether less experimental. They wanted to marry "Mr. Right," and they looked for a kind, thoughtful man who would be a good home-builder. In courtship, they liked soft music and soft lights and romance; highly dominant males frightened them and struck them as being brutal.

Low dominance women did not really like sex at all; they thought it was dirty, to be indulged in only for the purpose of producing children. They considered the male sex organ to be crude and ugly. (High dominance women found it beautiful.) They wanted the kind of man who would admire them from a distance.

One interesting point to emerge was that all women preferred a man of slightly higher dominance than themselves—not *too* domineering or he frightened them. In keeping with this, high dominance males tended to find medium dominance females sentimental; as to low dominance women, they might take them to bed, given

the chance, but they would never experience much personal involvement with them.

The alpha should have more than his fair share of children. But fortunately the children are spread fairly evenly across the dominance spectrum. The children of alphas are not necessarily top dogs, therefore, but they do tend to be more intelligent than average—because the alphas are more intelligent than average and this factor *is* inherited. As a result the intelligence of the group as a whole tends to increase; learning and experience should increase along with it.

From an evolutionary point of view this carries distinct advantages. It happens in animal communities but is unlikely to occur in a modern civilized human society, where too many artificial factors come into play—such as the fact that the alphas (who tend to be more responsible than other members of the group) probably practice birth control more efficiently than others and we can expect them to have fewer children.

Alphas are Often First-born

Strangely enough alphas often tend to be first-born sons. Again, this does not mean they will be more intelligent than their brothers and sisters, but it imparts a striving to succeed which seems to be characteristic of the eldest boy. This of course shows just what influence the parents' attitude can have. Most parents have a desire for their children to do well and the whole of their frustrations and desires tend to center on the first boy.

Research in the United States has shown that of those who were successful in a top level competition for an educational scholarship a very large proportion came into this category. The competition was so fierce that it demanded grit and determination—not just intelligence.

It becomes easier to understand when one thinks of intelligent parents kept down through lack of opportunity instilling their first-born with an obsessive need to do well; however, this determination, even coupled with exceptional intelligence, does not constitute true dominance which, as we have already seen, requires some of that magnetic leadership quality. Examination results therefore can never be an accurate guide to the degree of alphaness.

However, there is some real evidence that the eldest can be the dominant one. For instance, in the world of the kittiwake the female bird usually lays two eggs on successive

days and they hatch in the same order. The one that is older—by one day—invariably pecks the younger and becomes dominant. But this is not true in all animal groups. Among humans, however, the oldest son has been described as "power hungry." More still needs to be learned about this interesting quirk of birth order.

Age and seniority do play some part in the development of dominance, but what about sex? In the early psychological experiments virility did emerge as a significant force.

Experiment with Birds

Richard Adler quotes the following experiment: "Two flocks, one male, one female, each had its rank order. In the female flock the omega was injected with the male hormone testosterone, and in eight days rose to alpha. In the male flock the omega, similarly injected, rose as high as second rank. Maleness seemed an undoubted determinant."

And it is interesting that one female pigeon with the unprepossessing name of RY, who was right at the bottom of the social ladder, rose in six days for no apparent reason to third rank. Later it was noticed that she refused to mate and subsequently the researchers decided that some natural change had made her bisexual, had masculinized her to some extent. Hence her sudden rise in the dominance stakes.

Among hyenas, however, the female is the dominant one—she is also larger. Such a phenomenon is very rare in the animal world, but it does not seem to be merely a quirk of nature; it is possible to find a logical reason behind it. It is virtually impossible to tell a male and female apart even at close quarters because their genitals look almost identical—the female parts are swollen so they resemble those of her partner. Perhaps this indicates that she is naturally subjected to a masculinizing influence.

Of course, it is not as simple as that—especially among humans. Giving a man extra male hormone does not immediately push him up the dominance scale. But promotion of one man into the alpha position for whatever reason will automatically make him a sexually more successful person. An animal is more likely to be sexually confident and to be accepted as a sexual partner by the female if he is already an alpha. Most people will have noticed that the powerful men are the ones who get the girls. And the powerful women steal male admiration too.

It is interesting that women do not often reach the dominant position. Among women only, of course, they form exactly the same hierarchy as any other group of assorted individuals will do. But in the company of males the female rarely becomes the alpha—though she can easily dominate individual men. It may be because women, as a result of their vulnerable position in the bringing up of children, are programed only to follow men and not their own sex. The answers are not known yet. Of course women can reach the top and often do, but nowhere near as often as men and their lack of success is almost certainly not due solely to lack of opportunity or to brain washing during childhood.

Of course dominance is relative. In one group a fairly mediocre man can be tops—a big fish in a small pond; and a high quality alpha may still be low in the hierarchy in another type of milieu—roughly speaking he is a small fish in a large pond. What actually counts is the quality of the people above and below. If the people above the alpha are still more dominant, then an equilibrium will exist. But if those above the alpha are in that position only as a result of privilege and not through real merit then the alpha may become frustrated.

As a group, alphas vary greatly. There are ordinary alphas and there are high alphas—a rare breed who can do a great deal of good for the community—or bad. They are very special people and are tremendously important to society. Among them are the giants of the last war: Churchill, Roosevelt, Stalin and Hitler.

What benefits does alphaness confer on society? Dominant people are invaluable for many reasons. We already know that they reduce fighting within the group by maintaining order. By allowing a distinct leader and a hierarchy to develop, society has ensured its survival—for it enables a whole group of unequal, divided beings to act together for the good of each individual.

Feeling a bit ratty today? Well, according to latest research it may have to do with overcrowded surroundings. When many rats were caged in a confined enclosure, normal rat behavior, usually ordered and hierarchical, was replaced by extreme violence, cannibalism, and mob rule. The dominant king rat was the most violent of all.

Transworld

Transworld

Marriage & Women

Many women appear unhappy with the traditional marriage role. Why is their attitude changing?

Kim Sayer / Quartet

The marital relationship is arguably the most important one of all. It is virtually the only home-centered relationship in which a companion is *chosen* (there is not the same privilege with one's parents, siblings or children). Most significant of all, it is usually the longest-lasting relationship in one's life.

It is strange therefore that until fairly recently sociological researchers and psychologists have commonly regarded marriage as a major part of the life-career of a woman—but not of a man. They have tended to study only the wife's marriage: and still often do so.

In this they reflect the general view: that marriage is the concern of women; and that otherwise it is an incidental part of life—and a part that should be steady and unchanging, no matter how radically the society around it is changing. Most people experience a feeling of emotional well-being at the old-fashioned image of a good wife and mother: providing gentle care and encouragement for the more aggressive male as he fulfills his rat-racing, bread-winning and family-protecting role.

This seems not only an attractive arrangement for the husband and the children; it also seems a not unattractive arrangement for the wife. There is no more important "career" than bringing up children well; and there is, theoretically at least, no more exciting and fulfilling task than nurturing the developing intelligence and abilities of your own children, day by day. It seems a sane and creative role in a society whose values have eroded and decayed.

Yet great numbers of women are expressing increasing disenchantment with marriage after only a short time at it. They are not, they claim, feeling "fulfilled" by it at all. It seems that they would prefer going back to work to staying at home all day, even if they had only routine factory or office jobs. Why have so many women started feeling unfulfilled by housework and childcare?

The first answer is that the idealized wife is not only a rarity now, but probably always was a rarity. The long history of "nagging" women demonstrates this. A wife disillusioned with her husband may react in a number of ways but the commonest is nagging. If she wants to save his face (and her own), she nags him in private, but supports him in public. If she is reckless, she nags him in public as well. Nagging is the device of a dependent —someone who is frightened of being forced into the unprotected open, who is frustrated by her position but able to see no acceptable way out of it.

We probably also have a sentimentalized view of the close-knit "extended" family of old, with several generations in one house. Children married and moved to houses of their own, there was a high death rate among children, and a shorter lifespan generally. All of these seem to preclude such families being the norm. A larger number of children—and an even larger number of pregnancies—were common, however. And this made the role of wife and mother a full-time job.

The Failure of Staying Single

For today's wife, who most usually has two children, the shortest cycle of her marriage is that in which she has small children to care for; the largest is after the children have become self-sufficient —perhaps forty years. And nothing has prepared her for this long period in which she is all but superfluous.

In childhood and adolescence a girl is given to understand that she has a very short employment future indeed —just a few years to fill in until she is taken over by a loving husband. A boy is encouraged to think of his future in occupational terms. He will be an engineer, a journalist, or whatever. A girl is encouraged to think of her future identity as dependent on her future husband. In many different ways—directly and indirectly—she is told that "love and marriage" and a career are incompatible; and that failure to marry is the only failure a girl need worry about.

It takes a very determined, clear-thinking girl to resist this conditioning.

Unreal ads arouse impossible expectations about marriage.

Much of it is done with great tenderness, often by old or middle-aged men (including her father) who may look wistfully at the little girl, hoping that *she* may grow up to be the sort of gentle, unquestioning "wife-like" woman they had themselves hoped for.

As a result of such heavy conditioning, reinforced by magazine fiction and advertising and the media, the girl is likely to grow up with very unreal expectations of the roles she and her future husband will play in marriage. Her premarriage experience of men is unlikely to help much.

Courting customs have changed to some extent in recent years, with girls living in apartments of their own, and with many sexual prohibitions removed (often reducing the trauma of virginal sexual experience from the first weeks of marriage). But the traditional prerogative of the male still generally obtains: he does the asking. Since he also still usually pays all the bills when they go out together, a girl

today often leads a highly privileged life: earning herself, frequently on equal-pay terms, but paid for wherever she goes. This makes her very much a part of the affluent society.

A Reversal of Roles

When she is in love, and engaged to marry, she will have been courted, paid for, and waited on by the man. After marriage, the roles are more or less reversed. She usually keeps her job but becomes automatically responsible for the household chores. She is usually bewildered by their time-consuming nature and unnerved by the difficulties of learning to cook. Initially, though, she will wait on him with pleasure: she is in love, she is a new wife, she wants to be a good wife. She is, as it were, "playing house."

Research studies in Britain show that many housewives when interviewed will at first profess to like housework but then, after further questioning about individual chores,

The day your life became a dream...

The lasting beauty of EROS engagement and wedding rings will forever be a reminder of your happiest day. He means it when he seals it with an EROS ring. Come and choose from a full range of craftsman designed jewelry now!

EROS JEWELERS

Graham Marsh

139

Graham Marsh

will show that they dislike many chores, and merely "don't mind" others. This contradiction was most apparent among lower income housewives. Middle class housewives were franker about disliking housework. The lower income wives seemed unaware of the way they had contradicted themselves in the course of questioning: presumably the initial statement was an automatically defensive response about a role they knew to be generally despised.

Most wives come to resent the division of labor in marriage only if it becomes obviously unfair—if she is earning, for instance, but still has to do it all. Or, again, if her husband is not coming up to her expectations in his own masculine role: as decision-maker and protector of the family.

It sometimes seems that this is the commonest initial point of breakdown in the marital relationship. It is not that husbands are any less able nowadays: only that wives are less inclined to connive at a pretence that an inactive husband is all-competent.

This point of stress is demonstrated by a typical interview with three women, recently recorded by a journalist. Two were women in their late twenties who were beginning to find their marriages frustrating; the other was a widow in her seventies. The younger women were indulging in what she thought of as "Women's Lib" talk about their marriages. She was not so much shocked at this as amused by their naive attitude towards marriage.

One of the younger women was disturbed because her husband was avoiding making necessary decisions. She was, in her own words, "terribly feminine, I'm afraid: I _like_ the man to dominate." Her husband loved her "feminine" attitude, but in fact was not himself playing a sufficiently "masculine" role to support it. She kept trustingly leaving the decisions to him, but he had become increasingly irritable and evasive about each decision to be made—probably dating from a bad mistake he had made in an important decision early in their marriage. She was disturbed to find that she was beginning to nag him, in an attempt to get him to act. This made him accuse her of having "changed."

A Wife's Need to Share

The other woman, with a child away at school, had gone back to work and was strongly interested in her job. She continued to cope with all the domestic chores, as she had expected to do. But she resented the fact that her husband also expected her to continue playing a "feminine" role in other ways, like feeling interest and concern for him and his work, without expecting any return of interest or concern from him. Unlike the other wife, she rather liked to share in the decisions of the marriage, but she found that any divergence of opinion enraged him. At any point of difference he would angrily accuse her of an attempt to make him feel small and "inadequate."

Their husbands' reactions were inevitable, the 75-year-old widow told them with amusement. "You've got to learn to _manage_ a husband, without his knowing it." She proceeded to shock them both with a gaily cynical story of one of the times she had "managed" her husband into making a certain decision, while convincing him that it was he who was making the decision. Over a period of months she had systematically plotted their every conversation beforehand, lied, turned on tears at will, and discussed the plot with her female friends. She not only won her own way without his knowing it, but even, it seems, won his admiration when he finally realized the truth of the matter. "You _managed_ me over that business, didn't you!" she reports him as saying tenderly. "What a little manager you are!"

This Victorian concept of the feminine role in marriage was perhaps more hypocritical than at any time before or since. Of course, as research studies have indicated, many marriages today are run on similar lines. But both the younger women in this interview were shocked by the elderly widow's glee about her hypocrisy ("I respect my husband too much to treat him that way," they both agreed) and by her husband's apparent acceptance of it. And it is probably this unwillingness to plot and scheme, just to preserve an artificial sense of masculine capability in a husband, that is causing more married women to come into the open about their feelings about the division of roles in marriage.

The modern woman's increasing frankness is reinforced by the fact that she has enjoyed a period of financial independence before marriage (as her Victorian precursor would rarely have done), has probably traveled a little and generally looked after herself. She is still very dependent upon the precarious status of the married woman, however. (This is an odd status; it survives principally because _not_ being married is looked upon as total failure.)

Even if she is not still in love with her husband, even if there are no children to consider, she is unlikely to want to leave him or to risk his leaving her; there is no woman of lower status in our society than the woman whose husband has left her. But if he expects her to play a feminine role while failing to play the masculine one, she _will_ object.

Women unlike men are conditioned to accept short-term jobs.

Graham Marsh

Just as she has looked forward to being looked after, so most men in love look forward to the idea of their protective role as husband. Unfortunately there is no rule that says that every man—from factory hand to university teacher to millionaire—suddenly acquires husbandly abilities upon taking the marriage vows. The role of husband is the one managerial role for which no training is given.

In fact many a husband today must sometimes feel nostalgia for the relief afforded the husband by the diplomatic plotting of the Victorian wife. Modern marriage is far more demanding and realistic.

It is not that the average woman today wants to take over the managerial role in marriage. On the contrary, very often she does not even want equal "management." She is so heavily conditioned to the idea that in an attractive marriage the man will be stronger and more competent than the woman, and therefore the woman will be secure and free from anxiety, that she is usually very anxious to be able to admire her husband. She is, in effect, dependent upon him for her "identity."

The way in which she literally depends upon her husband for a new "identity" is the customary adoption of his surname. The purpose of this custom—to mark her as his property—has largely dissolved. She can own property of her own, can earn a living in a great number of ways, and so on.

Looked at objectively, it is an archaic custom, expecting a woman to relinquish the name she has had all her life until then. A new wife normally feels very tenderly towards her new name, as a symbol of her loved one and also of her new status. She is usually extremely glad to have discarded the "Miss" in front of her name—especially if she is over 30 years old.

Something in a Name

But since the syllables of our full name are probably the most significant syllables in any language, it would seem that the loss of half of this name must have a profound effect. Perhaps those who are least affected by the custom are the professionals who continue to use their own name in their professional life. Those who are *most* affected by it are women who are separated from their husband: then, using his name every day in identifying herself to people can be a disturbing reminder of the failure of that attempted new identity. Especially if her husband has left her, rather than

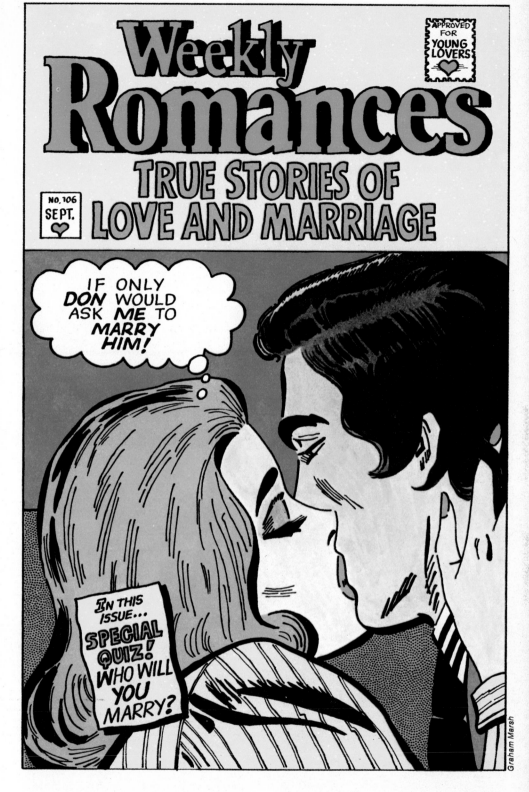

Graham Marsh

she him, this continued use of his name is probably damaging. Since reverting to her own name would mean endless painful explanations, however, she rarely attempts it.

For most women, even if very happily married, it is an extremely odd experience to hear her own name used by an old acquaintance who has not heard of her marriage. Hearing herself described as Jane Brown when she has become Jane Smith makes her feel almost as though she has been leading an expatriate existence,

Love will always sour for those who take romance magazines to heart.

and has now met someone from her home land. Often, in fact, a married woman can feel "foreign" to both identities.

Altogether, the institution of marriage is demanding archaic patterns of behavior from us. It is strange that through all the changes that have brought us from an agricultural to an advanced industrial society, and even through all the rapid social changes accepted in the mid-twentieth century, the concept of marriage has remained almost static, at least as far as the woman's role in it is concerned. All that time men have been railing against the unsatisfactorily "wifely" qualities of women, yet they have hardly considered adapting the concept of the allotted female role, nor even of adapting their own.

Now that increasing numbers of women are protesting about the unsatisfactorily "husbandly" qualities of men, perhaps we may eventually reach a happier compromise: each partner of a marriage might be willing to recognize that, as individuals, each is good at some things and bad at others, and perhaps both the chores and the "management" of the marriage might be shared out accordingly.

The marriage-role rules are set to fit the shortest part of the marriage-cycle: when there are small children, needing constant attention of the mother. Even at this time, they do not work very well. There is now a fair amount of sociological evidence that we have worked out our gender roles rather oddly. An American sociologist recently produced a volume of evidence from a variety of sources indicating that the people in the *worst* mental health in American society are the married women—and unmarried men. In *best* mental health are the married men and the unmarried women. There are of course many factors involved, but nevertheless, in a society that mocks the spinster as a total failure and lauds the carefree bachelor, this tells us a lot.

Although the divorce rate is soaring, thousands of people place their faith in computerized dating techniques to find a partner.

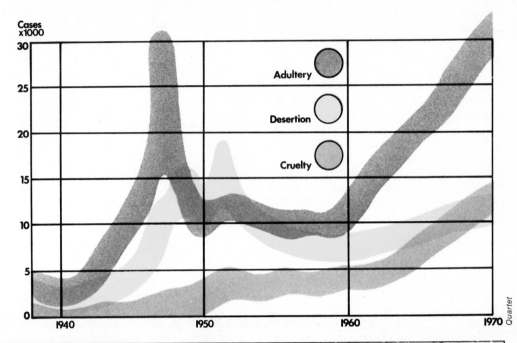

Fear & Superstition

No matter who we are, what we do or where we live, each and every one of us is superstitious to some extent. And whether this means avoiding walking under ladders or blessing friends when they sneeze, it arises from a sense of fear. Superstitions reflect our deep-seated belief in a kind of personal magic to ward off things we do not understand.

It has been said that man is a religious animal, but it could equally be said that he is a superstitious one. Throughout the whole of man's history an elaborate system of apparently irrational safeguards, often barbaric in character, has provided a foundation for much of his ritual life. The minor ceremonies which survive today in the form of superstitions are a constant reminder of the fact that man's mind has probably changed but little from that of his primitive ancestors.

Signs of Deep Anxiety

Many of these superstitions are apparently outward manifestations of deeply-seated anxieties. Their very existence implies an unquestioning assumption that there is some power external to man himself, which is capricious, tyrannical and highly dangerous, a force that must be cajoled and won over to one's side, or,

if it is hostile, kept at bay. Superstition is a form of personal magic for coming to terms with the unknown, a philosopy to which man resorts again and again whenever his modern gods fail him, when his faith wilts and he becomes afraid. Superstition offers the comforting assurance that it is possible to influence one's fate for good or evil by will power reinforced with ritual.

Such beliefs have usually been condemned as relics of outmoded ways of thinking, rather than as living expressions. More commonly the term has been used to belittle forms of faith which disagree with one's own.

Superstitions that have stuck. Third light on a match is unlucky—in war it gave snipers a chance to shoot. And fear of walking under ladders may have come from their early use as simple gallows.

Yet, any examination of contemporary superstitious beliefs indicates that these should not necessarily be written off as the result of errors of observation or reasoning, but should be considered as permanent traits of mind, the lingering thought processes of prescientific man.

Seven Years' Bad Luck

There is a primitive symbolism in the still-current superstition that breaking a mirror brings seven years' bad luck. The reflected image was originally regarded as the alter ego, or other soul, and damaging it was supposed to cause an injury to the person who had broken the mirror. To this mystical association we can attribute the growth of various luck-bringing measures, of charms and talismans.

Although to most people nowadays such objects have little real signifi-

cance, the modern charm bracelet, first introduced about a century ago, has found ready acceptance as a bringer of luck. The symbolic meaning of the particular charms is nowadays quite lost upon the wearer, who is conscious only of the fact that they are supposed to exercise a collective power to attract good fortune. To an earlier generation, each particular charm would have had its clearly defined function; the horseshoe, for instance, having the shape of a crescent moon, provided a safeguard against witches.

The most important characteristic of a luck bringer is the source of the power with which it is endowed. How does a piece of wood or metal acquire its status as a charm, and what are the channels by which superstitions are transmitted? One of the ways in which an object may acquire supernatural power is through association; thus a toy animal given to a child by its grandmother is regarded as an embodiment of her love and is a powerful luck bringer.

Two Basic Human Fears

Similarly, other superstitious observances spring from primitive reasoning. By false analogy a particular course of action which has proved successful in the past is associated with some object worn or action carried out at the same time, which is then accorded a mystic quality. The object or action is then used again or repeated, in the expectation of achieving a similar result at another time. Negative superstition, the avoidance of certain acts with the object of preventing undesired outcome, arises from a similar false association of ideas. In all this activity can be detected an awareness of some law of cause and effect, but it is the cause and effect of the savage, not that of the scientific man, the rule of assumption rather than thought.

Two human fears may be found at the root of a vast number of widely differing superstitions; firstly, fear in the face of change at the various crises of life, and secondly, fear of presuming upon the future, thus inviting the anger of the gods.

Of the two, perhaps the most dominant is that aroused by the prospect

Cat and crucifix. In many parts of the United States and Europe, the black cat is still considered the embodiment of the devil himself. A reversed crucifix placed around the neck of a black cat is thought to be a sign of evil spirits at work.

of change. It was for this reason that new objects and occurrences were in the past greeted with elaborate ceremonies designed to ward off the hostility of the supernatural powers.

Rites Before Birth

Among primitive peoples, the various stages of development in each individual from birth to death were always associated with protective devices, the vestiges of which survived until recently in the form of superstitions. With today's safer childbearing, many of the old birth taboos have disappeared, but some mothers-to-be continue to observe superstitious rites, such as those calculated to produce a child of the desired sex. A mother who wants a boy, for example, will wear a blue dress, and when hoping for a girl, she may still wear pink. The superstitious fear of presuming upon the future persists in the belief that it is unlucky to take the baby carriage into the house until after the baby has been born.

The onset of puberty was originally accompanied by magic rites designed to give protection against the hostility of evil spirits who were supposed to be particularly aggressive at this important period of life. The time has long since passed when menstrual blood was considered so threatening that a butcher would not permit his daughter to enter his shop during her periods, but it is still possible to find individuals who retain the belief that the sexual act carried out with a woman at such times can result in venereal disease.

No Image for the Bride

With marriage comes a complete change of direction in the lives of both partners, and the marriage ceremony is a veritable museum of old superstitions. Again out of fear of anticipating the future, the bride is careful not to see her image as a completely wedded woman in the mirror until she actually is so. If she has to take a last look before leaving for the church, she is careful to take off her glove. For the same reason, she will take care to avoid being seen by the groom before the ceremony.

Every feature of this important magical occasion has its particular superstitions; even the dressmaker who inserts the first stitch into the wedding dress can expect to be a bride herself before the year is out. Should the wedding ring, which is in effect a magic circle, be removed or broken it becomes ominous for the

marriage prospects.

Many primitive sexual superstitions have passed down the generations. Because the heat of the sun was once thought to be the source of life on earth, we continue to regard Mediterranean men as sexual athletes and Negroes as sexual dynamos. Because sexual activity was once regarded as a magical act, the seed or semen became sacrosanct; hence the long-standing myth that masturbation leads inevitably to a weakening of the physical powers, madness or even death.

Sickness and ill health, once the most feared of life's crises since they could lead to financial ruin, have lost some of their superstitious associations, thanks to modern medicine and welfare systems. Even so, to boast of excellent health is regarded as inviting psychic reprisals. The permanent fear of creating a situation by the mere act of referring to it by name is the real reason why certain diseases are mentioned only in hushed tones. For the same reason, the word death itself is often avoided.

Observances of Death

Even today death is associated with prophetic visions and mystical utterances; here superstition reaches its peak. The moment of death is signaled by stopping of clocks, pious drawing of curtains and the covering of mirrors. The mourner has entered "a special state of mind."

It is in the funeral ceremony that one observes an intensity of superstitious awe that no longer survives in the other areas of life. If the wreath has ceased to be regarded as a magic circle to contain the soul and prevent its return to haunt the living, it remains nonetheless obligatory even in cremations.

A crisis in the life of a nation, as in the life cycle of an individual, is the focus of superstition, and it is traditionally the onset of war which raises the tempo and intensity of irrational belief. During World Wars I and II a surprising number of superstitions which were centuries old suddenly received a new lease on life.

To paint the portrait of a battleship now became, to the seaman's mind, the equivalent of a sentence of death upon her. The jinx ship which is a commonplace of nautical life was discussed with even greater anxiety than previously. Sailors when about to embark upon a voyage considered it dangerous if a menstruating woman sewed a badge of rank onto a uniform. In 1914 German prisoners-of-war bore ancient amulets offering protection against death from bullets. In 1942 American servicemen carried iron-bound Bibles in their breast pockets for exactly the same reason.

Aircrews tended to resort under danger to a variety of death-defying fetishes, including amulets, mascots and lucky silk stockings, while their planes were invaded by those latter-day familiars, the gremlins. The belief in lucky and unlucky days was revived and one and all displayed a reluctance to presume upon the future.

Fervent Belief in Hunches

In peacetime, the degree of superstition which a man is likely to display is usually related to the riskiness of his occupation. Stockbrokers, whose financial lives are so often balanced upon a knife's edge of

Men will go to great lengths to protect themselves or to attract favorable circumstances. For centuries people in all cultures have used special charms, talismans and amulets to avert harm or to bring them good fortune. Such lucky charms gain a supernatural reputation because they become associated with success. In various ways fighting men often try to cheat death or avoid injury when they go into battle. For instance, World War II pilots had squadron emblems sewn onto their uniforms or painted on the fuselages of their planes. Some were given ferocious features like the Flying Tigers.

chance, have a strong tendency to consult clairvoyants, and American bankers are reputed to derive a sense of security from furtively touching the backs of passing hunchbacks! Out-and-out gamblers, whether at the roulette or card table, wear their superstitions almost as badges, displaying a fervent belief in lucky seats and hunches.

But the perfect example of a truly superstitious profession is the theater. The life of an actor is extremely insecure, and every theatrical production is a hazardous venture. In these circumstances many actors have a complete philosophy of superstitious practices, some of which must be as old as the profession itself. To stumble is an omen of forgetting one's lines. The final line of the play is never spoken in rehearsal as any anticipa-

U.S. Air Force

tion of completion is an invitation to disaster. If a long thread is found on an actor's back, it means that a contract is on the way. An actor will frequently treasure some little object associated with a successful first night's performance, regarding it as a form of magical insurance.

Another trade which was originally encrusted with superstitious usages is that of the seaman. In the days of hazardous sea voyages, the men on the big ships surrounded their lives with a complicated system of rituals and taboos. Today these superstitions of all kinds have dwindled.

On the other hand, among fishermen, whose lives continue to be at risk and whose incomes are precarious, the majority of older sea superstitions retain much of their original force. A skipper will frequently refuse to put to sea should he discover his hatch upside down on his boarding craft; a bucket lost overboard is still interpreted as a sign from the fates that the ship is doomed.

Objects of Special Reputation

All competitive situations, whether at work or at play, tend to create anxiety and therefore provide a solid foundation for the growth of superstition. In sport this principle is often paramount. The traditional belief that there is luck in odd numbers prompts bettors to place their money on threes, sevens and nines. Jockeys have their lucky caps, baseball players their lucky bats and some footballers not only touch the goal posts at the start of a match but have been known to prevent their wives from looking at the game on television.

In most cases a lucky object acquires its supernatural reputation because of its association in the player's mind with some important success in the field. The batter who makes a grand-slam homerun while wearing a particular shirt will often go on wearing it until it is almost reduced to tatters. Luck by association is the rule in sport as in all other kinds of activity.

A look at present day charms and beliefs makes it clear that superstitions move with the times, changing in outward form although never in essence. Motorists advance down the highways protected by lucky key fobs, and automobile salesmen are reluctant to deal in cars that have been involved in fatal accidents. Motor cycle policemen and Hell's Angels alike believe it unlucky for their crash helmets to be touched by alien hands. Civil air pilots and even astronauts are

Imperial War Museum

reported to take amulets with them on their flights, while the computer operator is coming to believe that his machine has a life of its own.

Superstitious fears are likely to arise in anyone—irrespective of social class or nationality—who feels himself threatened by forces lying beyond the range of his power. The form of a particular superstition may be determined by environmental and social factors, but the function of superstition itself seldom varies.

The Rites of Childhood

Children everywhere practice rites, some of them quite curious, to gain luck or to avert bad luck. And they will often not regard them as being particularly superstitious. In this way, children have something in common with primitive man who is naturally drawn to the mysterious and performs magic tribal rites.

The practices carried out by children to attract luck or to keep away bad luck are amazingly rich in complexity and variety. Many are practiced in fun or because "everyone does it," but others are regarded with dire seriousness.

For instance, children who see an ambulance will touch their collars and look about for a four-footed animal, usually a dog. They might also recite a magic rhyme, of which there are a number of versions.

Basically, the rhymes are all charms against the misfortune of being taken away in an ambulance. Sometimes there is a warning against swallowing until a dog is seen. The charm shields the reciter, their family, or even prevents the person in the ambulance from dying.

Another version of the belief says that the observer will have bad luck if they do not see a black dog soon after noticing the ambulance.

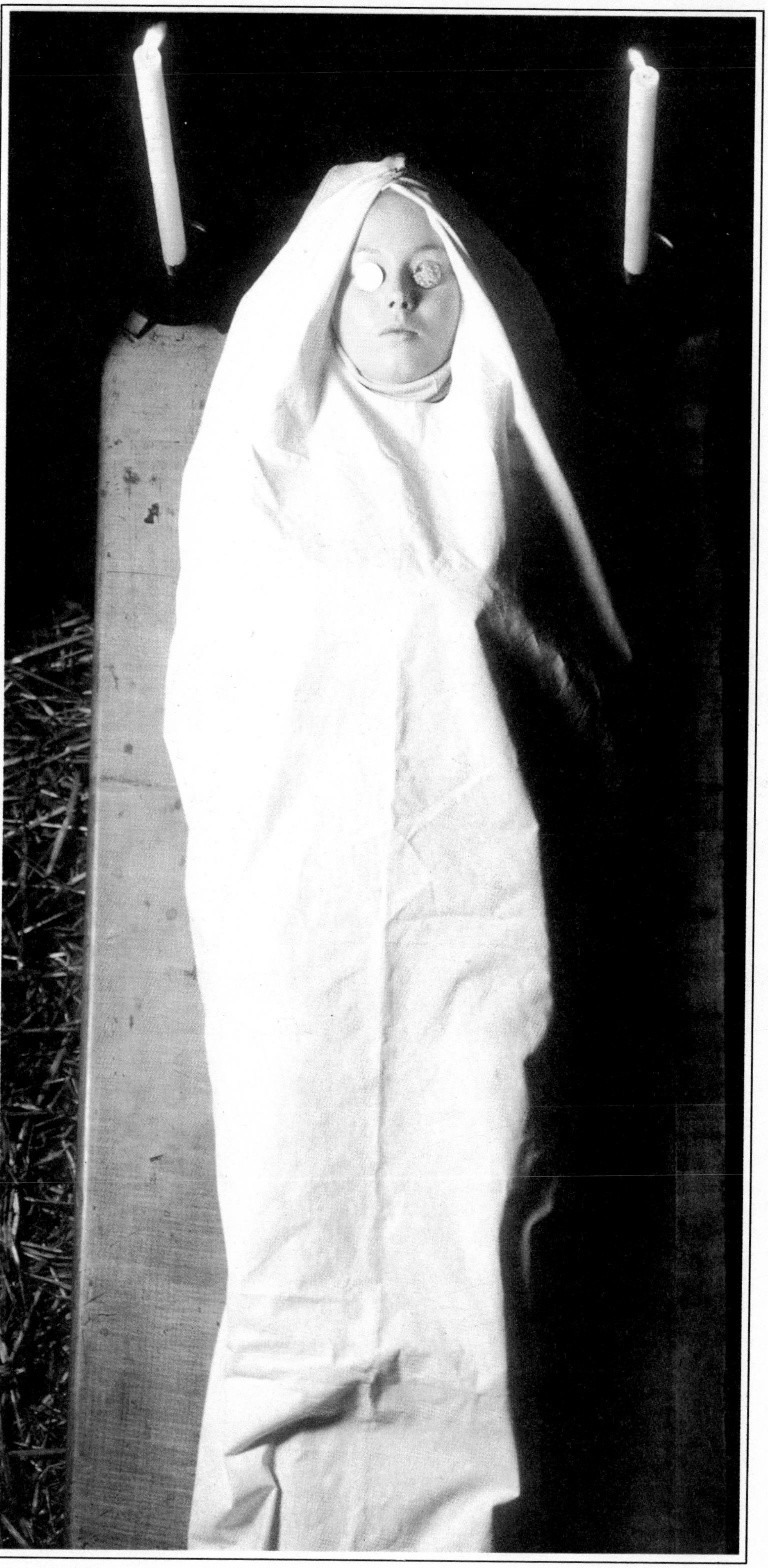

A corpse's eyes were kept closed with coins, which were also thought to be used to pay Charon, the ferryboat man who took the dead across the River Styx to Hades.

Transworld

147

All you want to know about…

psychotherapy

Q WHAT ARE THE MAIN APPROACHES TO PSYCHO-THERAPY?

A As the investigation of abnormal mental behavior has only been underway in systematic fashion for about a century, it is not surprising that there are major disagreements on the techniques and theories of psychotherapy. These, however, can for convenience be grouped into four headings, each representing special approaches, and yet at the same time each having a certain amount of overlap with others.

The two major headings are *individual* psychotherapy, and *group* psychotherapy. These should be almost self-explanatory, but in the first, treatment takes the form of a personal and private contact between the therapist and his patient, while in the second, the patient will be one of a group all of whom are interacting with the therapist in a particular session. On the whole, individual psychotherapy is the most productive since it allows the greatest rapport to be struck between doctor and patient, but it is a time-consuming process and is not necessarily the most efficient approach. Group psychotherapy comes into its own not only where there are large numbers of patients to be treated, but also in certain circumstances where a mentally disturbed individual can benefit from social interaction with other sufferers. A further subdivision of psychotherapy is into the *supportive*, and the *reconstructive* or *re-educational*. Both these approaches can be adopted in either individual or in group therapy. Once again there are no hard and fast rules, but supportive therapy is generally given when people are suffering from relatively mild or short-term neurotic conditions. Typically these might involve depressive bouts, feelings of insecurity or anxiety, mild cases of phobia and the like. In these cases, the therapist merely aims to reassure the individual, comfort him, and in certain cases offer palliative treatment such as drugs to relieve anxiety or sleeplessness. Reconstructive therapy on the other hand is aimed at longer term or more severe disorders, and the primary goal is to cause the individual, by one means or other, to alter his personality or restructure his psychology, so as to deal more effectively with the life challenges which have been proving too much for him. Psychoanalysis, incidentally, is one of these reconstructive approaches. Others include behavioral psychotherapy, client-centered therapy and existential psychotherapy, plus a number of less well-known or well-defined variants.

CAN HYPNOSIS HELP IN PSYCHOTHERAPY?

Yes, in certain circumstances. To understand exactly how, one needs to know a bit about what hypnosis is and what it is not. In brief, hypnosis is an altered state of mind or consciousness whose function is not properly understood but which places the individual in a heightened state of suggestibility or receptivity. In its deeper level the hypnotic state is vaguely like a trance or half-sleep. Body movement is stilled and the hypnotized individual behaves and thinks in a passive, relaxed way. It will be remembered that the basis of psychotherapy is to induce the individual to identify and resolve his psychological conflicts. Where the conflicts are superficial or readily identified, supportive psychotherapy is generally all that is required. But one of Freud's great discoveries was that people could be plagued by unconscious conflicts which were not approachable by a simple question-and-answer-discussion method. Hypnotized individuals, Freud discovered, were less evasive about their personal problems, and could apparently recall conflicts of which they were not aware in the normal waking state. Although the early promise of hypnosis as a key to releasing all unconscious conflicts has not been fulfilled, many therapists still find it useful in routine psychotherapy to help break down some of the barriers of inhibition which exist between the conscious and the unconscious worlds. To this extent hypnosis parallels the use of the mild sedative drugs in psychotherapy.

HOW CAN DREAMS HELP IN PSYCHOTHERAPY?

Freud described dreams as "the royal road to the unconscious." By this he meant that the dream reflected unconscious thought processes and made them available for inspection to the conscious mind. If one really wanted to know what motives and forces were driving an individual, and therefore also what were his principal conflicts and inhibitions, then one should study the material of his dreams, for it was here, he believed, that the unconscious revealed itself most clearly. For this reason many psychotherapists express great interest in their patient's dream life. Since not all dreams are straightforward, and many appear to be "symbolic" or "disguised," it becomes important for psychoanalysts to acquire skill in dream interpretation. Once the repressed motives or conflicts are revealed through the dream, the reconstructive aspects of psychotherapy can get fully under way.

CAN PSYCHOTHERAPY EVER BE HARMFUL?

Any technique can be harmful if it is misapplied. Psychotherapy in unskilled hands can be harmful if it builds up false hopes which are later dashed when the treatment fails to work. It can also be harmful if it is stretched out indefinitely to no purpose—though few reputable therapists would permit the process to continue if they felt the patient was not making steady improvement. Psychotherapy can also be harmful if it is administered improperly—e.g., if an individual with only mild and temporary problems is induced to undergo a major reconstructive course. Often people's personalities, if not perfect, are best left unaltered unless they are very unhappy with what they have to begin with! Finally psychotherapy can be harmful if it becomes an obsession with the patient. It is the duty of a skilled psychotherapist to make sure that his patient does not become overinvolved with the therapeutic relationship, so that he has little psychic energy available for the only too real problems—economic, social, educational, sexual, etc.—which the world outside the consulting room provides.

HOW LONG DOES PSYCHOTHERAPY USUALLY LAST?

It depends principally on the nature of the illness or mental disturbance, and also on the attitude of the individual himself to the therapy. Special skills and insights on the part of the psychologist also play their part obviously, but they are subordinate to the other two. The severity of the illness must be the main factor—some simple problems, such as depressions, mild anxieties, etc., can frequently be almost immediately ascribed to a cause and the patient can be helped to deal with the problems involved. Many common problems can be dealt with in only one or two individual sessions. For the majority of troubles however, a number of visits will need to be made, with an acceleration towards recovery once the cause or causes of the problem have been identified. Major personality disorders which require a restructuring of the individual's psychology and attitude to life may involve many sessions and effective therapy may occupy a year or more. In addition to the severity of the complaint, the attitude of the patient is of tremendous importance. An individual highly motivated to recover and responsive to the therapist's personality and approach will be far more likely to make a rapid recovery than will someone with a passive or negative attitude. The long time course of some psychotherapy is due to the fact that personality disorders are so great that the individual may have lost all motivation to recover and may even have withdrawn from the world altogether (as in some types of schizophrenia). Or he may be so deluded as to actively resist therapy by various subtle or unsubtle means. Orthodox psychoanalysis rarely takes less than six months and may take a year or more. Many analysts believe, however, that if substantial improvement has not occurred within a year, there is little hope of the therapy working and that the analysis should be abandoned.

ARE THERE SOME MENTAL ILLNESSES WHICH CANNOT BE TREATED BY PSYCHOTHERAPY?

A minority group of psychologists believe that most illnesses have a psychological origin. They base this view on the clear evidence that some physical illnesses—stomach ulcers, many skin complaints, and so on—are undoubtedly brought on or enhanced by stress and worry. Most experts however take the view that it is a small, though measurable, percentage of illnesses which are psychogenic (psychologically caused). At the other end of the scale there is a small number of experts who believe that the majority of psychological illnesses have a *physical* origin, and they support their position by referring to the evidence which has been building up in recent years, that some of the major psychoses (schizophrenia in particular) are caused by biochemical disorders and not by personal or psychological conflicts. Bearing in mind that the conflict of experts exists, one must nevertheless admit that some of the more severe psychoses do not seem to yield directly to psychotherapy. Perhaps this is partly due to the formidable communication barriers that exist between the psychotic patient and the doctor. But it is also hard to see how a biochemically caused illness could be expected to respond to conversation and to verbal attempts at personality restructuring. The psychoses excepted, most other mental illnesses can be treated with some success by psychotherapy.

IN WHAT WAY IS CHILD PSYCHO-THERAPY VALUABLE?

Psychoneurotic conditions, particularly those not caused by biochemical or other organic disorders, tend to develop as a function of age and increasing life stress. Most children, fortunately, lead relatively carefree lives for they are able to shift the burden of conflict and responsibility onto their parents. Occasionally of course this burden, for one reason or another, is not carried by the parents—there may be an emotionally unhappy family life, one or both parents may die, or the family may be too large, too poor or inadequately housed. Often children show great resilience to these stresses, though they may suffer in later life through feelings of insecurity. Others show insecurity and psychological disturbance as children, and it is here that child psychotherapy becomes useful. The topic is a complex one, but it can be summarized by saying that the role of the therapist is firstly to identify the conflicts and areas of stress which exist in the child's environment (often the most difficult job is in attempting to communicate with a withdrawn or unhappy child), secondly to offer the child guidance and reassurance whereever possible, and thirdly, consulting with parents or guardians, offering them reassurance and attempting to identify for them the problem areas. In many cases the situation distressing the child and inducing difficult or abnormal behavior is not hard to identify. The process of recovery may not however be a rapid one, and constant reassurance and guidance is often needed.

WHAT TYPE OF PERSON MAKES A GOOD PSYCHOTHERAPIST?

The first essential, though not necessarily the most important factor, is specialist training. In the case of psychiatrists this comes from medical school, for the psychologist from the university, and in addition for those who wish to practice psychoanalysis, the undertaking of what is known as a "training analysis." Other important factors are that the therapist should have a tremendous sense of tolerance and understanding, a personality tuned to the problems of others (though not so sensitively that he becomes depressed by them), an almost limitless fund of patience and the ability to inspire confidence in those who visit him. Some authorities argue that for a therapist to be really effective he should have himself suffered some psychological disturbance, and through psychotherapy have recovered. This, it is believed, gives him not only the necessary insight into the patients' problems and a genuine feeling of empathy with his position, but also confidence in the techniques which have helped him to restructure his life and which he now must apply to others. There is disagreement on this matter however, and some experienced psychologists believe that too much involvement and empathy can be harmful because personally committed therapists tend to see all illnesses in the light of their own condition, and thus are incapable of maintaining a detached and objective frame of mind.

HOW DOES GROUP PSYCHOTHERAPY WORK?

In most cases the ideal therapeutic relationship is a one-to-one contact between the doctor and his patient; just as personal tuition is generally the most satisfactory form of teaching.

The realities of psychological medicine (and the realities of education as well) mean that there are simply never enough trained specialists to provide everyone with a "perfect" one-to-one contact. Group psychotherapy, which might at first thought seem a rather unlikely approach to the problem, rose during and after World War II when large numbers of military personnel suffering from "war neuroses" were given supportive therapy in large groups. Military therapists found, somewhat to their surprise, that the group therapeutic approach for relatively minor ailments was highly successful. Since then it has been learned that the reason for this success was that the members of the group, by sharing common problems and being made aware of the fact that others were similarly afflicted, were able, to some extent, to offer each other comfort and reassurance. Another kind of group psychotherapy on this rather large scale is of course offered by the famous organization Alcoholics Anonymous, which achieves its sometimes remarkable successes by convincing alcoholics that they are in fact part of a large group who share a similar problem. With smaller groups, somewhat more specific and adventurous psychotherapeutic experiments are possible; one of the most interesting and successful has been the technique known as "Psychodrama," by which depressed, anxious and even occasionally psychotic patients apparently get some relief from their symptoms and insight into their conditions by "acting out" before a group of fellow patients the principal features of their illnesses as they see them. Psychodrama needs a skilled therapist in attendance, for many patients find the dramatization of their psychological problems to be filled with emotional stress. Group psychotherapy is at its most effective when it is used in a supportive role, and it can play only a limited part in reconstructive therapy because of the more serious disabilities of the patient.

Barnaby

Barnaby

Improve your observation

Have you ever had to give evidence about an occurrence, like an automobile accident? When someone asks you "What happened?" can you tell them clearly, with no doubt in your mind? It is not so easy as you might think. First, you may not have been ATTENDING to your surroundings, thinking about something else. Second, you cannot always believe the impressions you receive even if you are looking, because we often see what we expect to see rather than what is there.

APRIL
IN
IN PARIS

Most people do not even see the second IN.

Even if you both attended to and saw accurately what was there, there is the further problem of REMEMBERING exactly, and your memory can play tricks. It is quite rare for eyewitness accounts of the same scene to match completely. Look at the picture below for 30 seconds; if you have already looked at it, do not look again, but cover it and see how many questions you can answer.

1. What was the license number of the car?
2. Where was the car from?
3. What was the make of the car?
4. How many robbers were there?
5. Describe the men involved. Was there anything which might help identification?
6. What was happening farther down the street?
7. What kind of weapons did you see? Who is carrying them?
8. What was happening around the corner?
9. Describe the woman. Was there anything to help identification?
10. What was the sign in front of the next door shop?

Kim Sayer

When you have answered the questions, look back to the picture and check **Question 7.** What did you say to this? If you look closely, you can see that it is not clear that the other men have guns—yet many people jump to conclusions about the precise make of weapon, on the basis of insufficient information.

Question 9. This could be very important information, as the woman is part of the gang, pretending to faint to divert attention from the crime.

Question 10. This was a trick question—it is not really relevant to the main events. If you noticed this,

In a real situation, the shock and excitement of the event would make it a rather different experience from looking at a picture; this could work two ways, making you able to register

you could have a very good visual memory or you could be attending to too many small details to grasp the most important ones.

Score

8-10—very good; you would make a dependable witness.
5-7—good.
1-4—your observation is not so good as it might be.

more information, or interfering with clear-headed observation of what is there. The most important thing to do is to concentrate on the major events and try to "photograph" them in your mind, at the same time saying to yourself, for example, the car number plate. Rehearsing the information is as vital as noticing it in the first place. If possible, in a real situation, make notes soon afterwards. Otherwise your memory will alter and decay.

Perfect visual memory is a rare gift, but most of us could be more aware and retain our impressions better by concentrating, and by recalling the images and summarizing in words soon after the original experience.

Spot the Differences

Look at these two drawings for just one minute, picking out as many differences as you can. Then cover the pictures and write what you remember.

bar, cloud, windows in skyscraper, necklace, dress, pipe, tie, vest, glasses, and dress. How well did you do? Your powers of observation should be improving with concentration, new techniques for remembering, and practice.

Answers

There were twenty differences in the second picture. Reading from left to right and top to bottom: painting, sideburns, shirt, glass, earrings, buttons, belt, moon, building, window,

Miracle of the brain

There is no computer—no matter how sophisticated—which is as versatile, or as capable of complex learning, as the human brain, nature's greatest invention. And yet, this mass of pulpy gray matter, floating in liquid at the top of the spine, rarely weighs more than three pounds. We now understand at least part of its workings but there is still much of the mystery unsolved.

At the top of your spine, floating in a shock-absorbing liquid, and protected by about half an inch of solid bone, is nature's greatest invention, the human brain. If you are a woman, your brain weighs just under three pounds; if a man, slightly over. As women, on average, are smaller than men, the proportions are much the same for both sexes. In any case, brain size among humans is not very important. The largest human brain recorded weighed about six pounds, but it belonged to an idiot. What matters is what goes on inside it.

We actually know what this is, because the brain is the only organ that we know from inside. Its task is to make plans and to carry out actions. The plans and the actions that result are based on the information that the nerves bring to the brain about the world outside it.

Man is different from all other animals in that he alone is capable of complex and abstract thought. He has a "mind." Some animals do "plan" on a simple level. To get food, a gull will drop shellfish to break the shell, and a seal will even use a stone to do this. But only man will plow a field in January to eat in October; only man will ignore hunger feelings to observe religious fasts, or to stick to a diet, or simply finish something more interesting. The brain receives information from all the senses, decides what is important, and how to act. We have many possible "plans," even in the simple act of eating. It is the brain, not the stomach, that is in control.

Brain Waves

How does the brain work? We can find out something about the answer from the outside. If you shave some of the hair from the scalp and fix a tiny coil of wire on to the skin with a piece of adhesive tape, you will find that a minute voltage can be measured between the ends of the wire. It amounts to only about a ten-thousandth of a volt—you would need the current from about 40,000 scalps to light a flashlight bulb and about two million to light a household bulb—so the voltages have to be amplified if you want to record them.

If you do record them with a pen on a moving piece of paper, you will get a pattern of waves and zigzags, called an electroencephalogram (EEG). The method was invented by a German, Hans Berger, about 40 years ago. The pattern in some way represents what is going on in the brain, because when the brain changes its activity, the pattern alters. If you are resting, with your eyes closed, the moving pen draws a steady wave that goes up and down about ten times every second.

A cross section of the brain. The thalamus (4) and cortex (1) integrate incoming sense data; the cingulate cortex (2) aids emotion regulation and the corpus callosum (3) helps brain synchronization. The hypothalamus (5) governs many basic drives while the cerebellum (6) and the brainstem (7) control the muscles.

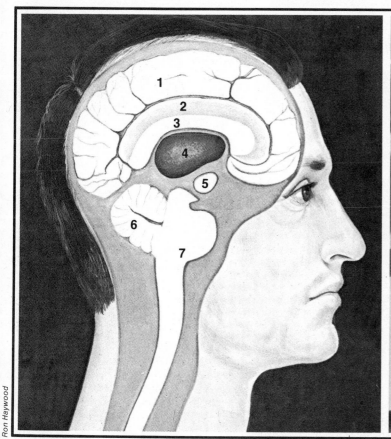

Ron Haywood

Pictorial Press

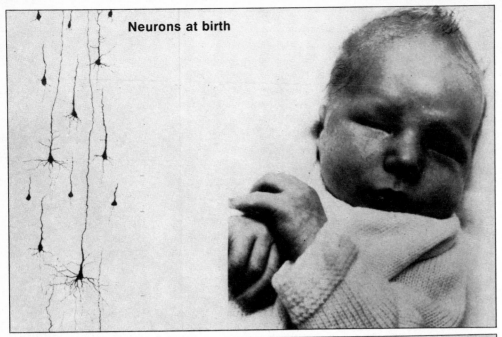

Neurons at birth

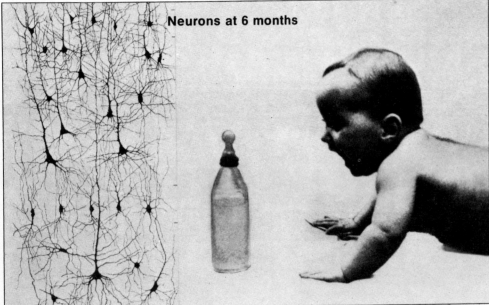

Neurons at 6 months

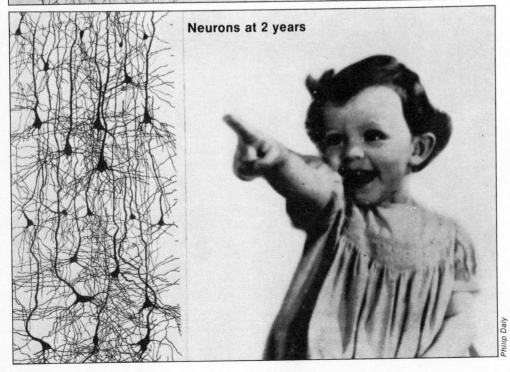

Neurons at 2 years

Philip Daly

This is called the alpha rhythm.

If you open your eyes, or are startled, or become excited, these alpha waves cannot be seen. Instead, there is a quick, irregular zigzag. If you fall asleep, the waves become slower and deeper. An epileptic fit shows up as a violent, wild surge of electricity.

Ticking Over

What do the patterns of brain wave represent? They show that the brain produces waves of electrical current. When it is ticking over, doing nothing in particular, these currents get into step, so that a wire outside detects a relatively large, steady wave. Once the brain goes into action, part of it is very busy. That is why the waves become small and jerky.

But even these small jerky waves are from quite a large area of the brain. No matter how careful we are, a wire outside the skull will pick up the waves from thousands of cells inside. It gives us only a crude idea of what is going on in the brain. It is useful for basic studies of sleeping, waking and excitement. If we want to find out more, we have to look inside.

If we were to open a human skull, in the way we open an egg, we would see a soft quivering mass, protected by a couple of skins. These hold the fluid that, among its other functions, acts as a liquid suspension to protect the brain from jolts. The skins curve over to divide the brain in half, and at places they are folded into tubes that carry blood.

The brain needs a very good blood supply. Although it has no muscles and cannot move, it uses an enormous amount of oxygen. A quarter of the total amount of oxygen used by the body at rest is used by the brain, and it is carried there by the blood. If this blood supply is cut for half a minute or so, you become unconscious. After about four minutes, the brain is irreparably damaged.

Farther in, below the outer skins, lies the brain itself, the part that thinks. If you start from the top, again as if opening a boiled egg, what you find first is a gray, jelly-like floppy mass. It is folded and crinkled and appears to

The human body possesses virtually all its neurons or nerve cells at birth. The newborn baby (top) has relatively few connections between neurons and the nerve cells still have to grow a little more. By the age of six months (center) complex tracery has developed and at two years (bottom) something like the adult pattern can be seen.

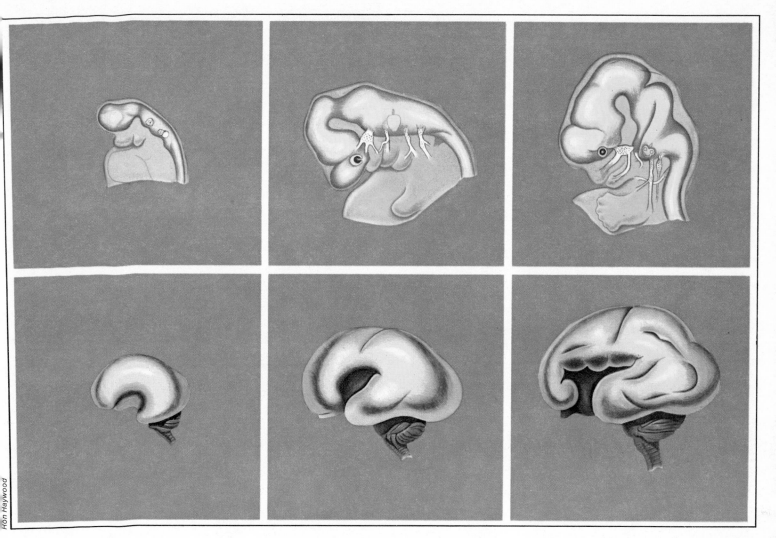

fill the skull, but if we could lift it, we would find two smaller sections of brain underneath.

The main gray floppy mass is called the cerebral cortex, and as we have a larger area of it, proportionately, than monkeys do, and as they, in turn, have a larger area than cats do, it is a fair assumption that this is the part that does the reasoning.

With a microscope, we can get some idea of how it does it. If we look at a thin layer of the gray surface, we will see thousands—billions in fact—of tiny spots with thin branching hairs attached. Each of these spots is a few thousandths of an inch across, and the whole cerebral cortex contains about ten billion.

They are the nerve cells—the *neurons*—and the cortex has to be folded and crinkled in order to hold them all. Because the branching hairs look like miniature trees, they are called *dendrites,* and the important clue about the way the brain works is that the dendrites from one cell mingle with those from others.

The cortex is about six inches thick and sits on a white mass. If we look at this through a microscope, we can see that it is made up of thick bundles

At each stage of the embryo (top) the brain (below) develops. Neural folds divide it into forebrain, midbrain and hindbrain. Then the forebrain grows larger and nerves link up to the spinal cord and body. Finally the organ develops into a brain of adult size and shape.

of fibers, each bundle wrapped in fat. The fibers are called *axons*, and it is the axons that carry the electrical message away from the nerve. The dendrites receive messages and the nerve sends its own message out along the axon.

The brain's job is to produce action that fits the situation that the creature —the human in this case—is in, and this action may be one of a long series that will eventually make some plan for the future work out. But the eventual function of the brain is to control muscles, and the control of muscles starts from the cerebral cortex. While we have the lid off, in our imaginary experiment, we can find out what muscles are controlled.

The odd thing is that this need not be an imaginary experiment. Surgeons sometimes have to open skulls to treat brain diseases, and they will

often do this with the patient conscious, using only a local anesthetic to deaden the pain of the cut. Although the brain itself is a mass of nerves, none of these have the kind of end they would need to feel pain or even a touch. In other words, you have no way of feeling if someone is touching your brain. Once the surgeon has reached your brain, he can experiment with it painlessly.

As we have seen, we know that the brain operates at least partly by electrical currents, because we can detect them from the outside, so one obvious experiment is to see what happens if we apply electric currents to the inside of the brain.

We can touch different parts of the cortex with a needle connected to a source of tiny amounts of electricity. As we move this contact around, we find that muscles move, fingers twitch, legs bend and straighten, and the eyes move from side to side. The patient is startled by these movements which seem to him to be "involuntary."

If we draw a map that shows which parts of the brain control the different parts of the body, we begin to understand one reason why man is outstanding among the animals. All movement is controlled by a thin strip that for right-handed people is on the left side of the brain. It runs from the top to about halfway down. At the top and inside one of the folds is the part that controls toes, ankles, knees and hips. Farther across are the parts that control trunk, elbow, shoulder and wrist. Then we come to the hand. An enormous part of the brain is involved —almost a third of the strip. This is why we can do so much, so delicately, with our hands: and our hands have no parallel in the animal kingdom.

What other differences are there? The obvious one is speech, and for speech to be complex, we need delicate control of the muscles of the jaw, the tongue and the lips. The strip in the cortex that controls these is nearly as large as the hand-controlling part.

Now we begin to understand how evolution has given man his present position. His brain has a large area, and has delicate control of the most important organs. But it is not much use having delicate control if the brain does not know what instructions to send out. This is where the rest of the nerve cells come in.

All the messages from the world outside the brain eventually reach the cortex, telling what is seen and felt and heard, for example. The brain then considers these messages, to see how they fit in with "its" plans. It has to recognize the objects and states described by the messages, relay them to one another, try new arrangements to see if they tell it more, and

In this section of cortex (left) are millions of neurons (nerve cells) like the one at the right. Incoming messages are passed through the dendrites or branches to the cell body, then along the axon or nerve fiber to be transmitted to other cells. Each neuron is interlaced with thousands of others for both reception and transmission of messages. These multiple connections turn a group of cells into an intelligent brain. At bottom is an illustration of how you hear and identify an incoming sound. The sound of a ringing telephone bell enters the ear in the form of air movement and travels to the ear-

drum. The eardrum transmits the movement of air to the coiled cochlea, which is buried deep inside the body's hardest bone. The cochlea encodes the sound and transforms its stimulus energy into neural energy. Neural or electrical impulses then move along the auditory nerves, carrying the encoded sound to the auditory cortex. In the auditory cortex the encoded sound is broken down into a recognizable noise. In the enlargement, a symbolic representation illustrates how the sound passes through one code filter and is noted as being harsh. Then it is identified as a ringing telephone bell.

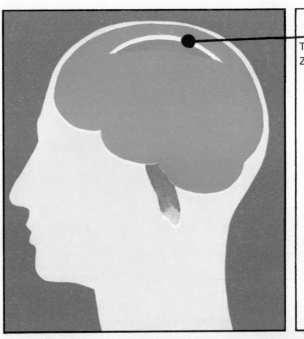

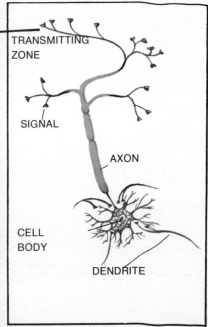

TRANSMITTING ZONE

SIGNAL

AXON

CELL BODY

DENDRITE

Gary Keane

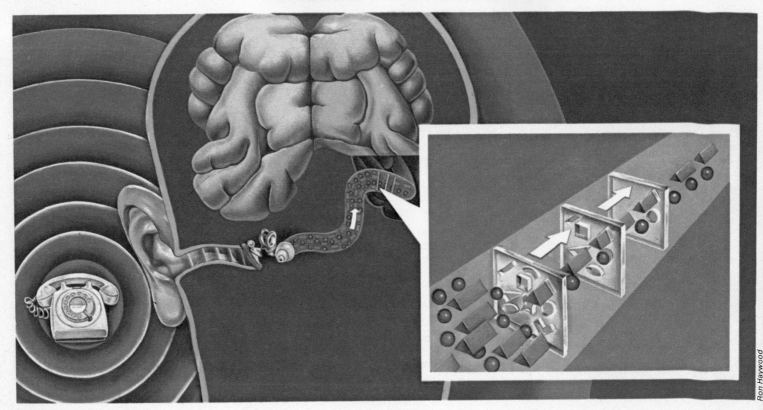

Ron Haywood

work out strategies for dealing with the situation. This is why the enormous number of nerve cells is needed.

We can consider lots of possibilities, and rifle through thousands of memories. To do this, we have about ten billion nerve cells in the cerebral cortex, and about ten times that number, a hundred billion, in the whole brain. We can look at an egg, and know that a bird will hatch from it, and be prepared to wait until it does. A cat can never have this foresight.

The Bee and the Window Pane

The shortage of nerve cells does not preclude an animal from having elaborate movements: it does stop it from being *intelligent.* A bee has only three hundred *thousand* nerve cells, compared with our hundred *billion* —in other words we have three hundred thousand times as many— but a bee can still gather nectar, build elaborate honeycombs and even, if the reports are true, tell other bees where to find flowers. But if a bee sees a flower outside a room and flies into a window pane in trying to get to it, it will fly again and again and again into the same pane. It will never try to find its way around, and will escape only with luck or help.

Sheer numbers of neurons are not enough. We often talk about the brain as a computer and even more about the computer as an electronic brain, and it is pointed out that the computer can never really rival the human brain because it must have far fewer parts than the brain has. You could hardly imagine assembling even a hundred billion transistors.

But this is not the main difference. In a computer, the input goes to a central processor that looks through the recorded memories, carries out some operations and then reports the result. Once the process is started, the computer cannot affect it. It simply carries out orders, which is why, if the orders or the information is wrong, the computer can deliver only nonsense. The input goes up one wire, or some equivalent, down another to the memory store, out again along another, and so on. The whole process is a long line of operations which eventually produces an end-product.

The brain works differently. The inputs of the nerve cells, the dendrites, in the cerebral cortex are interwoven and intertwined. They never work independently. What is happening to one affects those near it, and then those near the farther ones, and this means that any cell is affected by thousands of others. A message from the eyes reaches the part of the brain that interprets the message as meaning that there is wheat "out there" and this may activate memories which prompt that wheat has to be harvested and ground before it becomes food. This, in turn, might activate nerves that start the arm reaching for a sickle, but if a different set of images and memories is employed, the acting nerves might be those that start the arm reaching for a telephone.

It is only because we have this elaborate intertwining and interlinking of nerves that we can make elaborate plans and decisions with insight instead of a blind sequence of action. You might, just, be able to imagine a computer with a hundred billion equivalents of a computer—electronic engineers can make marvelously tiny components—but no one could connect them so that every computer affected every other one. Yet that is very nearly an account of the way the brain works. We can receive messages from all our senses and rifle through an enormous store of memories in the course of an action.

Input Intermingling

There are a few very simple actions, it is true. A muscle is kept in tension, so that, for example, we stay standing, by a nerve that senses slackening and another one that instructs the muscle to tighten, but virtually every other action is infinitely more complicated. A nerve from a sense organ will be linked to a hundred or so nerves, and each of these to a hundred or so more. These nerves have to adjust and correlate and inspect the messages they get and this is the main action of the system of nerves. Of all your nerves, 99.9999 percent are *adjusters*, as these intermediary nerves are called.

This is the secret of nature's greatest invention. It is the ability to intermingle the inputs from all the nerves so that all information is centralized. This is much more important than, for example, having delicate senses. Spiders have an array of eyes: we have only two. Moths can detect tiny traces of scents, using the twirly ends of their antennae, but the sense of smell in humans is poor, which is lucky, considering some of the places we live in.

But neither spiders nor moths, despite their delicate senses, can learn from experience. A spider builds a web across a pathway, and when it is knocked down, the spider builds an identical web in the same place. It can do nothing else. It has an inflexible program that it must follow. A moth, as we have seen, flies in a spiral path toward a flame, and if you save it from burning, it flies back to the flame again.

The Bulge at the Top of the Spine

These creatures have no brain, no center where all the information is brought together. The bee that lands on a glass window "knows" the window is there—its nerves tell it where to put its feet. But it cannot connect this knowledge with the fact that it cannot get out of the room, because different nerves are used in flying, and there is hardly any connection between the sets of nerves.

In fact there is so little centralization of what the senses "know" in these simple animals that spiders and insects do not notice injuries. A bee that has lost half its body will continue to feed.

The octopus is a slightly more intelligent animal. It can make simple decisions and learn to find food in a maze. But it still has very poor connections between its nerves. You can find out how easily animals learn by teaching them to associate food or mild punishments with particular objects. They will be attracted to one kind, repelled by the other. But you can teach one of the eight arms of an octopus to be attracted by a disk and another to be repelled so that bits of the octopus have learned contradictory lessons, and it takes a few hours for the lesson to be centralized so that the octopus acts as a single creature, with all its arms behaving in the same way.

If you think about it, you will notice that spiders, moths, bees and octopuses all have one thing in common, or rather they are all missing one thing. None of them have a backbone. No animal without a spine is very intelligent, because it is the spinal cord, the trunk lines of nerves that run up the hollow backbone, that takes messages to the brain, and takes its instructions back again.

The reason this system works so well is that the brain is not really separate from the spinal cord. It is the bulging end of it. As the child in the womb develops after conception, a tube forms. This will contain the spinal cord. A bulge forms at one end of the tube, and this enlarges to contain the brain. One end of the cord, in other words, specializes in interpreting and in making decisions. Nature's marvel, balanced on the end of the spinal cord, is actually the bulging end of the spinal cord itself.

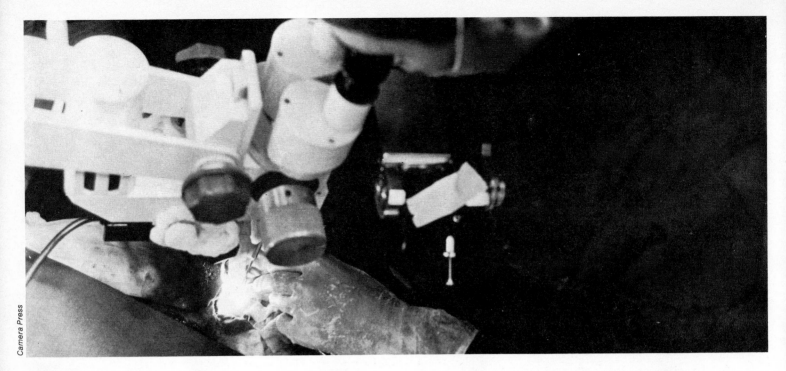

The brain at work

The brain is divided into three main sections: the forebrain, the midbrain and the hindbrain. Each of these areas controls different functions such as breathing, eating and remembering.

In a hospital in Montreal a patient in the operating room has a part of his brain exposed. He is also fully conscious because the surgeon has used a local anesthetic. It was the surgeon's aim to gently explore the surface of the living brain with electrodes, while the patient reported his experiences at each stimulation. The patient was a young man, J.T., who had recently come from his home in South Africa and the doctor was Wilder Penfield, one of the world's greatest neurosurgeons.

The electrical point at one stage touched a particular section of the right temporal lobe of his brain forcing the man to cry out: "Yes, Doctor! Yes, Doctor! Now I hear people laughing—my friends—in South Africa." After the stimulation was over and while still on the operating table he expressed his astonishment for it seemed to him that he was with his cousins at their home where he and the two young ladies were laughing together. This experience from his earlier life was as clear to him as it would have been had he closed his eyes and ears 30 seconds after the event and rehearsed the whole scene "from memory."

Does the brain contain a complete "memory" of everything that has happened to us? Although we cannot voluntarily recall everything is it possible that some forgotten experiences can be brought into consciousness with the surgeon's needle? Wilder Penfield believes that such a permanent record exists. Other experts disagree with him.

Memory is just one aspect of brain functioning which scientists have been studying intensively in the last 50 years and there are still no firm answers. What parts of the brain do what? Great ingenuity has been required to discover what we *do* know. We have learned much about muscles and sensations such as touch, and where in the brain these mechanisms are located, but we know relatively little about the complex processes involved in thinking and learning. It is possible that they are spread throughout the brain and not specific to one area.

Let us first examine what we do know.

The brain resides in the skull or cranium and is connected at its base to the spinal cord. In the developing fetus it is formed from tissue known as the neural plate.

Segments of the neural plate become the forebrain (at the front), the midbrain (in between) and the hindbrain (at the rear). The nervous tissue which eventually becomes the spinal cord is contained in the hindbrain.

The three tissue layers which cover the brain and the spinal cord are known as the meninges.

The outer layer, the thick *dura mater*, lines the skull. Two thinner layers, the *arachnoid mater* and the *pia mater*, come under this, next to the brain and the spinal cord. Between the two inner layers there is a substance called the cerebrospinal fluid. This fluid covers both brain and spinal cord.

Man's brain, and indeed the brain of all vertebrates, is divided into three regions: the forebrain, the midbrain and the hindbrain.

The forebrain consists of the cerebrum, which is divided into two cerebral hemispheres and joined together by the corpus callosum; and such structures as the thalamus and hypothalamus.

The hindbrain includes the cerebellum and the pons, a bridge of connecting tissue between the two hemispheres of the cerebellum and the medulla (an enlargement of the spinal cord).

The midbrain is the intermediate zone between the forebrain and the hindbrain.

In man, by contrast with primitive vertebrates like fishes, the cerebrum is enormously developed: the cerebral hemispheres take up about 80 percent of the human brain. It helps, in looking at the functions of the brain, to think of it in three concentric layers — a primitive core at the center; an older brain which evolved upon this core; the outer layer of new brain. Of course, all three layers are closely interconnected in a very complex fashion.

Let us first look at the central core which includes part of the hindbrain, midbrain, thalamus and hypothalamus — i.e. much of the brain stem. The bodily functions most vital to our existence — breathing, eating, mating — have their origins here, and in this region, concerned solely with the necessities of survival, such basic emotions as contentment, anxiety and terror find their roots.

Brain Functions

The *thalamus* is a pair of egg shaped bodies and it is the major relay station of the human brain. Except for smell, almost every sensation we experience converges on the thalamus where the information is analyzed before being relayed to appropriate areas of the cortex. Thalamic sensation is intense and unrefined. A person whose sensory cortex had been destroyed would find that the thalamus makes such mildly unpleasant sensations as cold unbearably uncomfortable.

The thalamus also has something to do with fear. Dr. José Delgado reported how one of his female patients responded to electrical stimulation of the thalamus. Her face immediately took on a fearful expression and she turned to either side, visually exploring the room behind her. When asked what she was doing she said she felt a threat and thought that something horrible was going to happen. The response started with a delay of less than a second, lasted for as long as the stimulation and did not leave any observable after effects.

The *hypothalamus* is located deep in the center of the brain. Its chief function is to control such life maintaining processes as body temperature, respiration and blood pressure. In situations of stress it prepares us for action by increasing the heartbeat and sugar levels in the blood. The hypothalamus may also have something to do with our emotional reactions.

If a certain part of the hypothalamus of a cat is stimulated electrically there will be a spectacular outburst of aggression. The hair bristles, the pupils of the eye open wide, ears lie back and the cat hisses and strikes out viciously and aggressively. It also controls our

basic drives of hunger and thirst. By surgical excisions scientists have been able to eliminate all sense of hunger in rats so that they die of starvation even though food is readily available to them.

The functions of the thalamus and hypothalamus are closely related to that of the neighboring *reticular formation*, a collection of neurons with short connections to other neurons lying in the brain stem. The reticular formation has much to do with controlling the state of arousal as in changing from sleep to waking or from diffuse awareness to alert attention. Damage to a portion of the reticular formation in an animal produces one which sleeps much of the time and whose brain waves show the patterns characteristic of deep sleep.

Around this central core of the brain are older parts of the brain that serve somewhat more complex functions. These structures are commonly called the *limbic system.* Located deep in the forebrain the limbic system is composed of the amygdala, the cingulate cortex, the septal area and the hippocampus. In conjunction with the hypothalamus this system can exert profound control over our emotional behavior.

Emotive Points

Neuroscientists have found that the *hippocampus* for example has something to do with memory storage. Patients who have had this pair of bean shaped organs removed because of disease can remember clearly events in their lives that occurred before the operation, but they cannot remember anything new for more than a few moments.

Such a case, known in medical history as "H.M.," is an American who in 1953 at the age of 27 underwent a brain operation for severe epilepsy. During the operation his hippocampi were severely damaged. Since then H.M. has lived from minute to minute. Since his operation he can remember nothing except for a few minutes at a time. If he meets someone with whom he spent the day before he has no recollection of the meeting. He will read the same copy of a newspaper over and over again with fresh interest each time.

The *amygdala*, which is positioned against one end of each hippocampus, connects directly with the hypothalamus and in some way influences its level of emotional output. Damage to the amygdala can excite animals to extremes of rage or hypersexuality — or can make them com-

pletely docile and harmless.

One experiment concerned a female patient, an attractive 20-year-old girl who was given to fits of unpredictable rage and was therefore committed to a mental hospital. Aggressive behavior similar to her spontaneous outbursts of rage could be induced by electrical stimulation of a certain point of her amygdala. The point was stimulated while she was enthusiastically playing the guitar or singing.

Pleasure Center

At the seventh second of stimulation she threw away the guitar in a fit of rage, attacked the walls, and then paced the floor for several minutes. Then she gradually became more quiet and resumed her normal cheerful behavior. This effect was repeated on two different days. This information was, of course, of great significance in treating this particular patient's problem behavior.

The *septal region*, located deep in the frontal lobes, seems to have something to do with pleasurable sensations, particularly of a sexual nature. In one study a man suffering from narcolepsia (periodic attacks of a sleeplike state, lasting minutes rather than hours, from which a patient may be aroused with or without difficulty) was given electrical stimulation in the septal region of the brain. He reported that this made him feel good, as if he were building up to a sexual climax, although he was not able to reach orgasm. He was anxious to repeat the experience.

These basic brain functions, controlled by the primitive core and the older brain, are arguably more necessary to survival than the complex reasoning and motor centers in the cerebrum. They are the life-sustaining functions that continue without conscious thought (how inconvenient it would be if we had to think every time we took a breath!) and allow man time to reason and remember.

Bumps of Destiny

Man's all-consuming interest in where his head is at is as old as history itself. Archeologists have found the skulls of men who walked this planet over 10,000 years ago with holes deliberately bored through the bone structure of the skull. Trepanning as this practice is termed is thought to have had a religious significance — perhaps an attempt by ancient man to increase the sensory input of the brain by further inlets. How successful these somewhat drastic measures might have been is difficult to say but

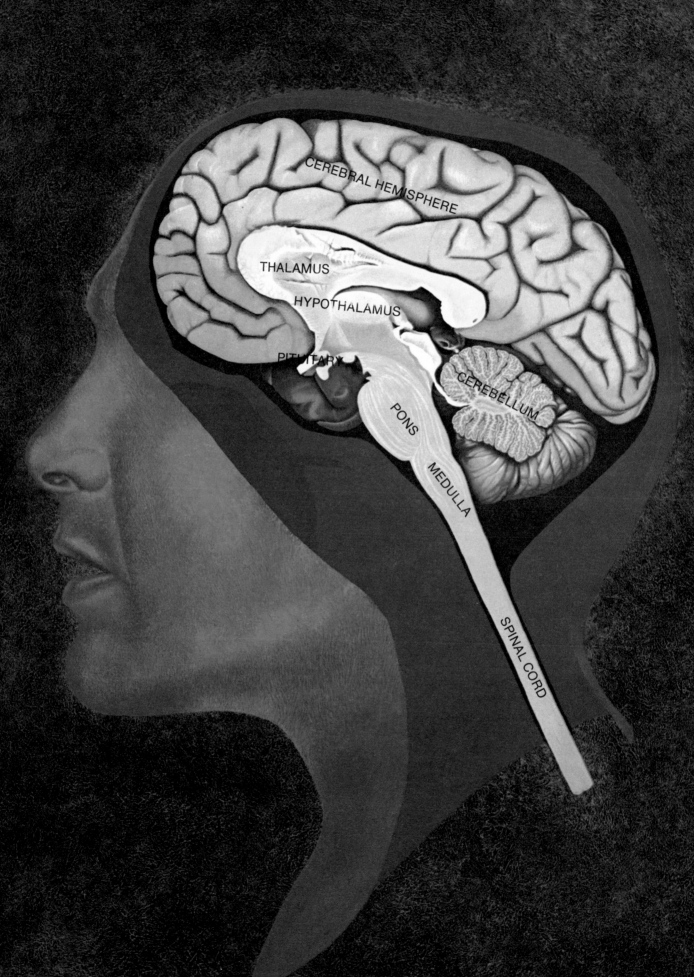

certainly the subjects lived to tell the tale for some skulls clearly bear the marks of having been trepanned twice.

Phrenology, of course, is not concerned with the alteration of the cranial structure but rather with its observation and deduction of personality from cranial topography. It originated with the work of Franz Joseph Gall (1758-1828)—a German physician who was the first man to use his gray matter to point out that while the white matter housing the brain is merely the supportive tissue to the active parts inside, its contours also give clues to intellect and personality.

Headmaster

Gall thought that the shape of the brain (and therefore the head) is related to mental capacity and that different parts of the brain govern different parts of the body. Modern neurologists have shown the truth of the latter at least and today it is recognized that one region of the brain controls the hands, another the feet and so on.

But Gall went one step further, arguing that abstract qualities and tendencies such as pride, courage, greed, and firmness have specific locations in the brain. Thus phrenology came to hold that a man's character is determined by the interaction of various "organs" of the brain, the size and power of which can be detected by the trained phrenologist from the bumps and dips of the skull—much as a geologist reads the landscape by the contours of the map.

By feeling a certain area of the cranium, the expert it was said could tell for example how well developed his subject's "organ of combativeness" was and thus could decide whether his was a passive or an aggressive personality. Physiognomy was an extension of this principle assessing human personality according to physical features of the entire man, believing that the outward formation of any part of the body would

The adult brain comprises 10,000 million nerve cells which consume 25 percent of the blood's oxygen supply. The two cerebral hemispheres covered by a layer called the cortex seem to control our higher thought processes. The thalamus absorbs all incoming information while the cerebellum works below the level of consciousness as the coordinator of the human body. The limbic system, deep within the brain, appears to govern specific functions, e.g. emotional and sexual arousal.

Phoebus Photo

give an indication of the inner man beneath.

Gall's ideas were systematized by his disciple, Johann Spurzheim (1776-1832). The science of phrenology spread rapidly through Britain and France and by the 1830s there were at least a dozen British societies in existence. In America phrenology also became all the rage and phrenologists traveled the country giving exhibitions of character analysis. Soon everyone with a pair of hands and a phrenological chart was at it and the skull as well as the bank balance of every aspiring bachelor was carefully scrutinized by a prospective mother-in-law.

"Happy marriage," advised one Victorian marriage guide, "is promoted when both husband and wife possess a full development of Amativeness (the projection of the lower and back part of the head behind the ears). Men who possess large Amativeness combined with development of friendship and strong vitality enjoy the company of the female sex intensely while those who have small Affirmiveness rather avoid the society of women and sometimes evince a want of refinement, respect and delicacy of feeling in their intercourse with them."

Gall's system was constructed purely by observation. Having selected the place on the skull of a suspected faculty he examined the heads of his friends and casts of persons with that pecular trait in common. The spirit of combativeness for instance was verified by examining the head of "a quarrelsome young lady."

But phrenology as proposed by Gall and Spurzheim could not last, for as medical science progressed to the tabulation of the various parts of the brain so the rather vague generalizations of the phrenologists fell into disrepute and the craze for phrenology waned and passed away. The debt modern brain surgery and psychology owe to the early phrenologists, however, is large, for their work did much to stimulate research into the anatomy of the brain even if the maps and charts of the head contributed very little to the understanding of the human psyche.

Phrenology studies human nature through the contours of the skull. It was all the rage in the nineteenth century and many skulls showing how to read the bumps and dips still exist. An electric phrenometer went a step further charting exact maps of the head.

But if phrenology has become a discarded "science" many ancient phrenological beliefs have been preserved in our everyday language. Here are some of the old wives' tales about your head. Big headed? Well are you, literally? If so, traditionally this indicates that you have a tendency to be somewhat proud and headstrong while conversely a small head may be a sign of an introverted personality.

Skulduggery?

And those of you with high foreheads will be gratified to hear that almost universally among old wives this has been considered a sure sign of intelligence from whence no doubt we have derived those curious phrenological phrases, highbrow and lowbrow.

And what about going soft in the head? Part of the skull of every newborn baby is very soft and only hardens as the child matures. And it is also true that in old age there is a tendency for the skull to soften, perhaps an indication of a second childhood or an inner simplicity sometimes apparent in old people.

It would follow from this line of reasoning that anyone who was rather dull and uncomprehending might be termed "thick-headed" or "numb-skull." It all seems remarkably logical somehow . . .

Perhaps phrenology cannot just be dismissed as the practice of quacks skilled in skulduggery. It is just possible, from recent research, that it may, after all, provide a few of the answers to some major headaches about the brain. The twentieth century has seen a great revival of serious scientific interest in the possible effects of physique on character. In 1921 the psychologist Ernst Kretschmer published a study of mentally abnormal people in which he attempted to tie up their physical structure with the type of their mental disease.

More recently William Sheldon has divided humanity into three broad physical categories, ectomorphs, mesomorphs, and endomorphs, each group exhibiting broadly similar traits of personality. It is interesting that this classification corresponds to that made by some phrenologists into "mental," "motive," and "vital" types.

Science is just now learning to take a backward step and give credit to the wisdom of earlier beliefs. It is unlikely that phrenology is one of these, but if your hands have strayed to your scalp and your interest in phrenology has been aroused, maybe it would be unfair to say you need your head examined!

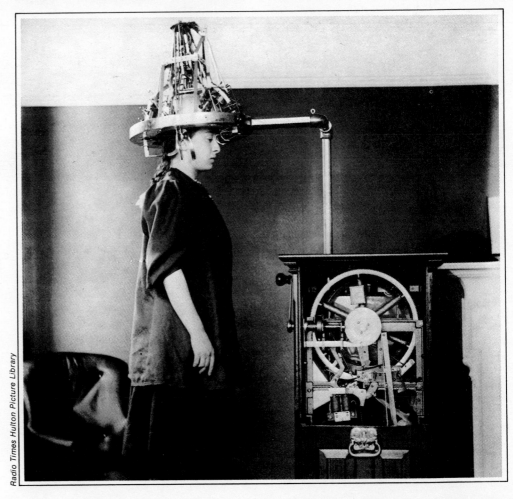

Mission control

Man is capable of precise and intricate acts like hitting a ball, playing the piano, or making himself understood through speech. All such acts require reasoning and coordination and we think we understand how the brain governs them. But we have only just begun the voyage of discovery into the inner space of the mind. Going further into outer space may prove the more easy task.

By far the most vital and interesting part of the brain is the cerebrum, which controls our reasoning. It is situated at the top of the brain and consists of two large hemispheres. These cerebral hemispheres are apparently mirror images of each other. For the most part, functions of the right side of the body are controlled by the left hemisphere and functions of the left side by the right hemisphere. However, the chemical or structural differences in the hemispheres mean that in right-handed people the left hemisphere controls intellectual performance and the right hemisphere controls perceptual performance. In most left-handed people this is reversed.

The two hemispheres are connected by a fiber knot called the *corpus callosum*, the main function of which seems to be helping to synchronize the activity of the hemispheres. Each hemisphere is divided into four *lobes*: the *frontal* lobe, the *parietal* lobe, the *occipital* lobe and the *temporal* lobe. From these lobes the body's functions are initiated and controlled.

Movement

At the back of the frontal lobe lies a strip about an inch wide which commands all the muscles of the body that produce movement. When a patient is conscious during a brain operation the surgeon can give electrical stimulation in this *motor strip* and produce definite movements: an arm movement, a knee jerk, a shoulder shrug. Patients so stimulated have no control over their movement. Indeed they are often surprised when it happens.

One patient, according to Dr. José Delgado, tried unsuccessfully to stop a hand-clenching movement produced by electrical stimulation and remark-ed, "I guess, doctor, that your electricity is stronger than my will." Wilder Penfield, the Canadian brain surgeon, and his colleagues in Montreal have mapped this motor strip in detail through electrical stimulation.

In the parietal lobe is another strip which lies parallel to the motor area—the sensory strip also explored by Penfield. This area controls sensory experiences, as when a part of the body is being touched or moved, or subjected to extreme heat or cold. A person with disease or injury in this area may lose his sense of touch or his ability to tell the positions of his arms or hands when his eyes are closed.

Vision

At the very back of each cerebral hemisphere in a part of the occipital lobe is the area important in vision. New research on the visual cortex has

shown that when spots of light, or slits of light, are presented in different positions the cells within the visual area respond differently. We perceive not simply points of light but form and movement as well. Electrical stimulation of this main visual area will cause a conscious patient to see lights, colors, and shadows. It is this kind of external stimulation which causes us to "see stars" when we are given a jolt to the head.

Hearing

The auditory area of the brain is found on the surface of the temporal lobes at the sides of the hemispheres. When this auditory cortex is stimulated the subject variously describes the sound as ringing, humming, clicking, rushing, chirping, buzzing, knocking and rumbling.

Speech

As early as 1861 the French neurologist Paul Broca examined the brain of a patient with speech loss and found damage in an area on the side of the left hemisphere. This area has

As you see and hear this performance, your body reacts to the physical impact of light and sound. The music beats its way into your brain — the rhythm pulsing through your veins, your heart beating faster, and your eyes reflecting the flashing lights. The sound seems to have possessed all of your senses.

since been known as "Broca's speech area" and to it have been assigned the functions of motor speech, that is control of the tongue and jaws in speaking. The usual interpretation is that this area is located in the *left* hemisphere of right-handed people, while it is found in the *right* hemisphere of left-handed people.

But speech is far too complex to be localized in this simple manner and psychological disorders of speech and language (aphasias) have defied simple classification. In the late 1950s Wilder Penfield and Lamor Roberts in Montreal made a close study into which parts of the brain were essential for speech. They found three areas on the left side of the brain which are

concerned with the content and meaning of language, as distinct from those parts of the brain which look after the mechanics of voice control.

The brain mechanisms for hearing and understanding words are different, by the way, from those for hearing and understanding music. The Russian composer Shebalin, for example, produced his best work after a stroke had robbed him of his ability to understand speech. The stroke was on the left side; music is usually dealt with on the right.

The Interpretative Cortex

We have high foreheads. Our primitive ancestors had lower brows, and the monkeys' are lower still. You could guess that human memory and reasoning go on in the frontal lobes behind those arching skull bones. And you would be wrong.

Some time ago an accident which happened to Phineas Gage, the foreman of a gang building a road, showed what the frontal lobes do *not* do. The road had to be blasted through a hill; a hole was drilled, a charge of powder

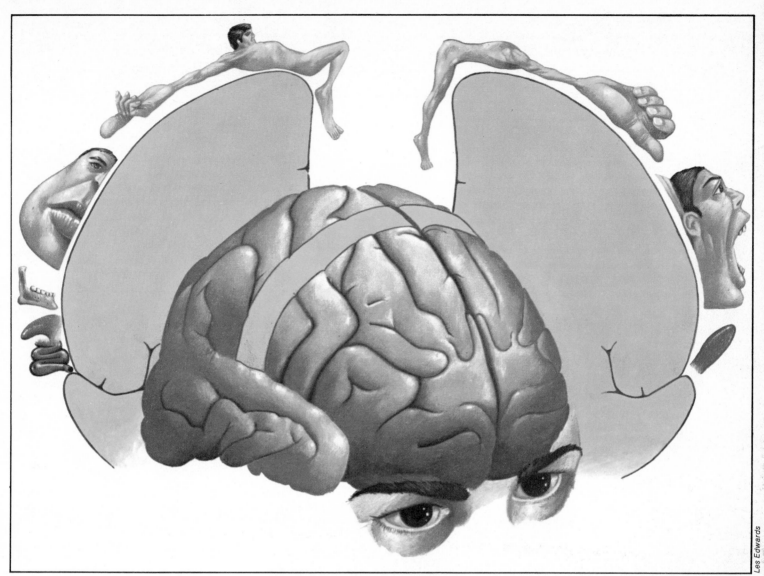

Above is an artist's conception of the motor strip, a brain area of about an inch wide that commands all muscles which produce body movements. Shown here opened out, the strip on the brain's left side controls the body's right side, the converse being true. But each side has some control over its own side of the body. It should be noted that a larger proportion of nerve cells is devoted to the fingers, which need precise motor control, than is given, for example, to the trunk. And the lips are allocated more area on that side also. Aside from other parts of the body, the right side of the strip, also known as the somesthetic cortex, commands the jaw and tongue in speaking as well as the intestines and abdominal region. The left side of the strip or the motor cortex controls, among other functions, the lips, jaw, and tongue in swallowing. At right is a view of an actual brain from the rear, which has been split down the middle, showing its internal formation in a more realistic representation.

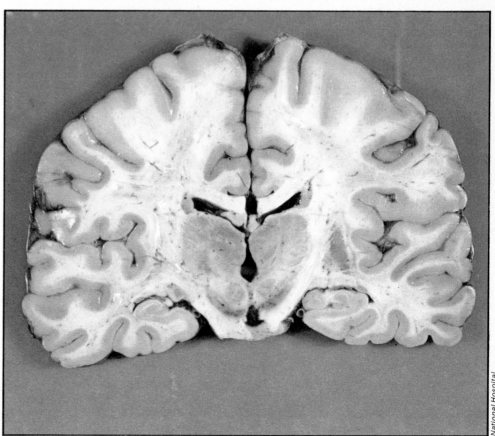

Les Edwards

National Hospital

put in and covered with sand, to control the explosion. Phineas Gage, by accident, tamped down a charge that had not been covered, and it exploded. The tamping rod, 4 feet long and 1½ inches thick, was driven through the front of his head.

Gage was stunned by the wound, but eventually came to and walked to a doctor. He described perfectly clearly what had happened, and the wound was cleaned with antiseptics. It healed, and he lived for another dozen years.

His left frontal lobe was badly damaged, the right one slightly, but what was totally unexpected was that Gage's memory seemed normal. His reasoning functioned normally as well, and he could have continued as a foreman, so far as his intellect was concerned.

But as far as his personality was concerned, he could not. Before the accident he had been considerate and efficient; now he was ill-natured and capricious, and, after a while, no use as a foreman. Eventually he earned a living as a curiosity on exhibition.

In Phineas Gage, at least, the frontal lobes had little to do with memory and reasoning, but accidents like this are rare under normal circumstances, and it was years before much more was found out about what the frontal lobes did. The clues came from injuries in World War I, and although none of these injuries was so dramatic as Phineas Gage's, the total of the evidence was valuable.

Frontal Lobes

It was found that whatever happened to the frontal lobes, the patient still breathed, his heart still beat, and he digested food. These "automatic" processes are certainly not controlled by the frontal lobes.

The patients retained their memories and they lost none of their physical skills. Sometimes they did worse on intelligence tests but occasionally performed better. They *were* consistently worse in tests where they had to make complex decisions in abstract situations.

So, except for this somewhat higher mental activity, intellectual tasks do not need the frontal lobes.

The minds of patients injured in this area worked more or less as before, but the personalities were changed. Ambitious people lost their drive. Considerate people became insensitive and even bad-tempered. And many of the patients became casual and happy-go-lucky, without a thought for tomorrow.

The frontal lobes, it seemed, were connected with the personality and the next experimenters tried removing these lobes from chimpanzees.

If one of their frontal lobes was removed, there was not much effect. If both were taken out, the chimpanzee had difficulty only with what were for him complex intellectual tasks.

Lobotomy

This discovery did not have much value to psychiatry but one odd result did. One of the chimpanzees was bad-tempered, and eventually became too awkward to use. Dr. Carlyle Anderson, at Yale, removed both frontal lobes, and she became relaxed and cheerful, but less competent.

Egas Moniz, a Portuguese neurosurgeon, hearing of this, developed the technique of "frontal lobotomy" as a treatment for mental illness in humans. The procedure involved severing the nerves that connect the prefrontal area with the rest of the brain—and for this he was awarded the Nobel Prize.

In fact, it became a badly abused medical practice. Many of the patients were dehumanized. They were often reduced to clever animals with no determination, careless of the results of their actions, apathetic. A lawyer who asked for a lobotomy was worried because he got violently drunk from time to time. Afterwards he still got violently drunk—but he no longer worried about it. The misuse and tragic results of lobotomies have been dramatized in American novelist Ken Kesey's book, *One Flew Over The Cuckoo's Nest*. Today it has been virtually abandoned as a treatment for insanity.

But despite the fact that the front of the brain has important bearings on personality and foresight its precise functions are still unknown. It remains the most mysterious part of the human mechanism. Electrical stimulation of the frontal lobes usually produces no activity comparable with the rather dramatic results from stimulation of other parts of the brain.

Neurosurgeon Wilder Penfield gives uncanny narratives of what happens when the temporal lobes of the brain are stimulated. Very often such stimulation evokes random flashbacks into the patient's past. One patient heard a familiar song so clearly that she thought that a record was being played in the operating room. Another patient exclaimed, "Oh, a familiar memory—in an office somewhere. I could see the desks. I was there and someone was calling to me—a man leaning on the desk with a pencil in his hand."

To the patient these flashbacks seem very vivid and for Penfield they are evidence that the brain retains a complete and permanent record of the stream of consciousness.

The brain then is an instrument with specialized parts. But its primary usefulness as a center for many kinds of circuits is its ability to choose, coordinate and integrate. We know some of the ways in which it operates, but after a decade of intense study many basic questions still remain unanswered.

We can never be certain that our theories of how the brain works are scientifically correct—they are only hypotheses. To say that our brains are like computers does not mean that we understand them—we are still just on the threshold of comprehending the implications of computers. Electronic brains or computers are merely calculators and cannot, as yet, meet the sophisticated standards set by our own brains. And computers cannot tolerate a mistake, whereas the human brain absorbs errors as a matter of course. Mistakes can bring a computer to a standstill, yet spur the human brain to ingenious alternatives.

Fiction to Fact

Now we are trying out methods that will allow a machine to "think" in the human sense. The work is limited by our imperfect understanding of how we think and react to stimuli. But the basic idea is that thought is pure mechanism, and that anything which is pure mechanism can be reproduced by machine: We have already developed computers which can play chess or checkers in a superior manner but it is said the programs are not quite up to human standards.

Scientists are also trying to copy intuition, that most human of our attributes. But it would appear, after a study of results so far, that a breakthrough in the mechanization of thought processes is hopeful only in a simple sense. Yet there is a chance that we will develop machines that could be made as intelligent as we are or that could reproduce our thought processes entirely. Eventually this may happen. Then our whole idea of control over machines would alter and so would our way of life. We may one day find that it is our minds which are out of date. The next step is to make new brains of greater scope than our own and this opens up a whole new world of more than science fiction.

Big Brother is Watching Over You

Our brains have programed us for survival. Have you ever wondered what makes your heart pound and your breath come faster when you run upstairs? Great bursts of energy like this consume large amounts of oxygen in the body's cells and your brain is simply using one of its many amazing automatic mechanisms to replace it.

Rapid breathing infuses fresh oxygen into the bloodstream while increased circulation rushes it to the tiring muscles. All this is done immediately, without a moment's conscious thought, by a control system scientists call cybernetics.

To most of us, the word cybernetics rings of computers, space travel and robots. But actually this is a concept firmly rooted in nature and involves any stable system—physical or mechanical—which maintains, through self-control, certain specific conditions.

Put simply, it is the same kind of regulation that keeps an electric oven at a steady temperature. As long as a heat detector built into the oven registers a certain temperature, there is no need for more heat; but as soon as the oven falls below, say, 325° a mechanism is triggered to start the heating process again, and is activated whenever the temperature falls below a set standard. The message of heat deficiency is termed *negative feedback*, and it is as necessary to the system as the switch that turns on the heat.

It is surprising how often this principle occurs in our lives. The human body incorporates a great many negative feedback controls, and several of these are found in the brain. One such center is the hypothalamus, located in the central core of the brain, which among other things regulates body temperature.

If the hypothalamus receives negative feedback indicating temperature deficiency, it can do several things: it can increase production of heat in the muscles through shivering, and it can decrease the diameter of the blood vessels near the body surface so that the heat from the blood is conserved in the center of the body, where it is necessary for survival. This lack of blood supply to the skin is why people go white with cold.

If the negative feedback indicates the body is too warm, then the hypothalamus increases evaporation of liquid from the skin (sweating) and it increases the diameter of the blood vessels near the body surface, giving overheated people a flushed appearance.

Another important control is the respiration center, located in the medulla oblongata at the base of the brain. This is what governs our breathing rate and is sensitive to messages which indicate when too much carbon dioxide is in the blood. To get more oxygen to replace the deadly carbon dioxide, the respiration center makes us breathe faster and more deeply.

This is why a mountain climber in a rarefied atmosphere with low oxygen content or a man who has just run upstairs will have to breathe at a much greater rate than normal. It is also the reason we automatically gasp for breath when we come up from swimming for a long time under water. Only an act of will overrides this reaction and prevents us from breathing under water, within certain limits that is. Eventually, conscious control must give way and we breathe in water and drown.

Naturally, the person who breathes water dies just as surely as the person who does not breathe at all. The point is that we cannot help reacting in this way. We breathe, no matter what the consequences, whether we are under water or in the fresh air.

Usually, of course, the fact that the will cannot inhibit our regulatory reactions keeps us alive—this is what they are intended to do. For instance, a child in a temper tantrum holds its breath until it turns blue. The terrified mother usually gives in to the child, but if she would just wait a minute, the child would faint from lack of oxygen and then, once its perverse will power is made inactive, begin to breathe again. Nature will not let us die quite so easily!

All cybernetics means is that if a certain—usually unfavorable—situation exists, a specific set of reactions will occur to inhibit and control it. This is the principle that engineers have borrowed to build highly complex computers.

Many robots, for example, are equipped with a photoelectric cell which produces a small electric current. If someone or something gets in the way of this current, a mechanism is triggered inside its "body" and the robot miraculously moves.

A robot call Rosa was once built to interact on stage with real actors in a production in a London theater. She played the Queen of France—truly a "command performance."

The most complicated computer is based primarily on the self-regulatory systems in our bodies. Though machines like this appear amazingly intricate, they are child's play compared to the human brain.

Marshall Cavendish

Delgado:
Mapping the mind

Macabre though it sounds, our bodies can be controlled merely by someone pushing a button. The brain makes the body obey its commands by sending out a series of electrical currents. If electrodes are implanted in the brain, these currents can then be controlled externally.

The bull snorted and then charged the moving man. But a dozen yards from the target it skidded to a halt and looked around in confusion. All its aggressive instinct was gone.

The bull's target had been Professor José Delgado. And he had just demonstrated how it is possible to control a bull by accurately implanting electrodes in its brain.

When the bull came at him, Professor Delgado merely pressed a switch on a radio transmitter tuned in to the electrodes, throwing the animal into confusion and robbing it of aggression.

With the transmitter at "off," the bull returned to a normal state of mind, pacing the ring, snorting and looking for another man to charge.

The brain is the control center of the body which it commands by sending out instructions on tiny electric currents. These can be detected from outside the skull. Psychologists record these currents when they are investigating diseases of the brain. If electrodes are put into the brain, they produce electrical currents and it is then quite easy to influence the brain's command structure by remote control. It is a surprise, at first, to discover that these electrodes can be used to produce what seem to be conscious emotional states, but which are, in fact, merely responses to electrical stimulation.

We need to understand emotions for the practical reason that some

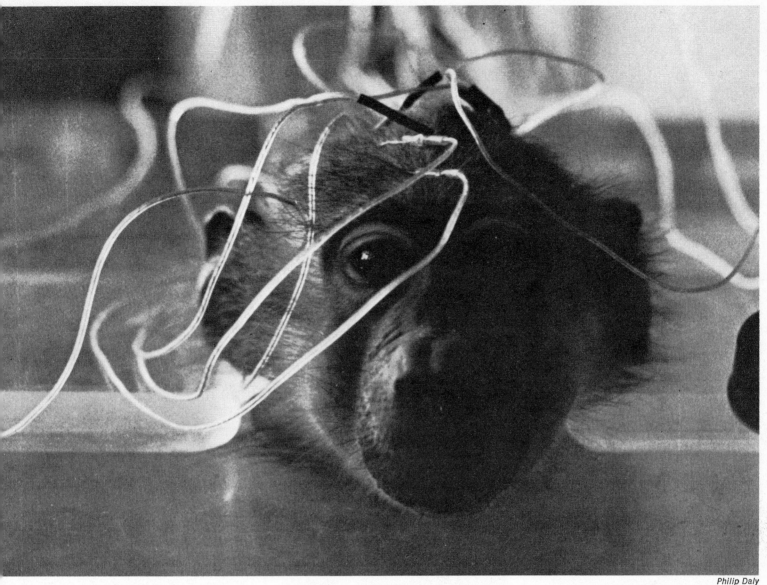

Philip Daly

people's emotions are so disturbed that it causes them suffering. Other people have emotions, such as aggression, that are powerful and anti-social. One way of studying emotions is through experiments with electrical stimulation of the brain, and this has been a life-long pursuit for Professor Delgado.

Fighting bulls have a limited range of emotions, and while switching off a bull's aggression is striking, it would be more useful to know how the emotions of animals closer to us are controlled. For this purpose, the best experimental animal is the monkey.

In principle, the tests are easy. The monkey is anesthetized, and a small hole is drilled into its skull. A metal electrode with a wire fixed to one end is carefully slid into the monkey's brain so that it touches the part to be stimulated. The hole is plugged with dental cement and the wire fixed to the skull.

In recent experiments, the electrode is directly connected to a tiny radio receiver which can be implanted in

Slap-happy rabbit (left). An electrode wired to its brain stimulates a "pleasure center." The rabbit will become addicted to the button that activates the electrode in preference to eating or mating. Much information about the brain has been gleaned by the use of electrodes which have been worn by monkeys (above) for a number of years.

the skull, so that the skin and hair will grow over it. The monkey cannot feel the electrode, because there are no "touch-sensing" nerves inside the brain. The electrode itself is made of stainless steel or silver or platinum, which will not be affected by the natural fluids inside the brain. Several monkeys have worn their electrodes for long periods—four years or more. For many experiments more than one electrode is necessary, for each one reaches only a tiny part of the brain. Some of Delgado's chimpanzees carry a hundred electrodes each.

An odd fact about electrical stimulation of the brain is that the animal

or person being tested cannot feel when the current is switched on. His arm or his leg moves, and he will seem surprised to see it moving, so in some cases it is very difficult to consciously control the rest of the muscles to cooperate with the one that is being artificially controlled.

One of Delgado's monkeys, Kuru, had an electrode put into his brain. When the current was switched on, Kuru stopped eating, and walked around his cage, avoiding all obstacles. When the current was switched off, he sat down and started eating again. The experiment could be repeated every minute for an hour without apparently upsetting Kuru.

Complex Movements

It is simple to make a monkey twitch a leg or move its head by transmitting a tiny electric current to the receiver it carries, but this does not really relate to actual behavior. Producing a complex movement is more relevant. Walking, for example, uses about a hundred muscles, in the legs and ankles and feet and trunk and arms and even the head, and they must all operate together if the animal is not to fall; yet the complete order, "Walk," is controlled by one tiny section of the brain.

The fact that there are centers in the brain through which complex movements can be artificially controlled is startling enough; but the emotions that underlie these actions are even more interesting. There is one obvious difficulty in trying to study emotions in animals, for the only visible manifestation of an animal's emotions is the behavior aroused by by them. It is tempting to suppose that the animal is feeling what the observer would feel in a similar situation. It is easy to believe, wrongly, that when a monkey is smiling it is happy.

The first person who induced offensive behavior in a cat was careful to say that it acted "as if threatened by a dog." When an electrode in the cat's brain was switched on, the animal spat and hissed, its hair stood on end, and it unsheathed its claws. However, at first sight these actions provide no real clue to the animal's emotions.

Two Kinds of Rage

But through careful observation it is possible to make a very shrewd estimate of what an animal's behavior signifies, although it becomes more complicated in light of certain experiments. For Professor Delgado has found a way of producing both a "sham rage" and a "true rage." An electrode switched on in one part of a cat's brain produced what was only a show of rage. The cat hissed, and its hair was erect, but it did not attack any other cat. When another cat attacked it, it lowered its head and flattened its ears in submission.

But an electrode in another part of the brain could produce real rage. The cat roamed its cage looking for a fight, but carefully avoided the biggest cat. When it found a foe, the cat crept up on it and fought it "rationally," fitting its tactics to whatever the attacked cat did.

What Delgado had found here was a part of the brain that switched on aggression, which then expressed itself in the way the cat chose. This behavior in fact bears a rough resemblance to sudden aggression in humans.

Experiments with monkeys tell us something about systematic aggression within groups. A group of monkeys—a colony—is a small society. One monkey becomes the boss, claim-

ing most of the territory, feeding first, and taking first choice of the females. There is usually one other male who is his chief rival, while the others grade themselves in a social order.

There are certain points in the brain of the boss monkey that make him aggressive; these can be found by experiment and electrodes can be put in. When the current is switched on, the monkey becomes even more aggressive, chasing and biting the others. The fascinating thing is that this is not simply meaningless rage; it is controlled aggression and is perfectly integrated with the other "values" of the monkey. The boss directs most of it at his chief rival.

This monkey was only exaggerating his normal actions, but even a retiring monkey can be made aggressive with an implanted electrode. Lina, a female, was bottom of her group of four. She had the smallest territory, she was last at the food, and all the others

bullied her. The behavior of the other monkeys was altered until Delgado had a group where Lina was second of four, the chief rival to the boss. Then Delgado switched on the electrodes he implanted in the aggression center of her brain for five seconds every minute for an hour. Lina started to attack the other monkeys and was particularly vicious to the boss. The boss did not dare fight back. Lina briefly became boss, but retired to her number two position when the current was switched off.

Living creatures are not neutral jellies, waiting to be excited and declining to a passive state once the excitement goes. Every muscle has an opposing muscle that returns the limb to its position, and every emotional impulse is kept in check by one that opposes it. If there is a part of the brain that switches on aggression, there must be another part that switches it off, and if this center

Keystone

Throughout the ages the lion has symbolized man's aggression. The violence of some football fans, for instance, makes a striking parallel, perhaps indicating that aggression is not emotionally or socially based as was once thought but is governed by purely physical stimuli.

could be found, there would be some way of understanding and perhaps dealing with the excessive aggression of violent criminals or, for that matter, of violent policemen.

Carlos, one of Professor Delgado's chimpanzees, was temperamental—most chimpanzees are. He disliked being teased and he resented strangers, but he liked playing with people he knew. But when an electrode carefully placed in an "anti-aggression" center was switched on, anyone could touch Carlos and stroke him. He was friendly with everyone. Everything in his behavior was normal, except that

his aggression was curtailed.

The effect was even more striking in a monkey colony. A monkey named Ali was the boss of this group. He was so firmly established that he only had to threaten the others to subdue them. He would look at them while biting his thumbnail, and they would leave the food. At a glance from Ali the males would creep away from the females and leave them to him.

Delgado found the correct place in Ali's brain and fitted an electrode to it. When this was switched on, Ali became quieter and could be stroked. But the experiment went further: Delgado put the switch for the electrode _inside_ the cage. Monkeys are inquisitive, and eventually they tried the switch. Elsa, one of the submissive females, discovered what the switch did; she found out how to make Ali less aggressive, and whenever he threatened her she would run to the switch and turn it on. She never be-

came boss monkey, but she cleverly learned how to have a peaceful, unthreatened life.

Monkeys' brains have control centers that turn emotions on and others that turn them off; these can be interfered with by using electrodes; and they also have centers for the more complex feelings.

If you stroke a cat, it purrs. It shows pleasure—it will rub against you and settle down for more stroking. Pleasure, like aggression, is controlled in the brain. There are no nerves in the cat's skin that distinguish agreeable sensations, for if we stroked it very quickly, or stroked it against the way its fur lies, we would affect the same nerves in the cat's skin, but the cat would not show any pleasure.

Enjoyment by Training

Presumably it would not feel any. Somewhere farther along the nervous system, in the brain, there is a nerve center that decides that it will "call" a certain group of sensations pleasure. Thus the brains of animals, and even human beings, can be trained to enjoy what others would find painful.

. If an electrode is implanted in a particular part of a monkey's brain and the switch left near the monkey he will quickly learn to press the switch to produce a reaction of pleasure in the brain, yet there has been no external stimulus ordinarily associated with approval or enjoyment. If the electrode is correctly placed, he will press the switch a dozen times a minute, hour after hour, and he will prefer the pleasure the electrode gives to any other. He will ignore food, even if he is ravenously hungry; he will ignore females. And yet if the switch is disconnected, the monkey becomes "normal" again, eating when hungry and mating when aroused.

What these experiments all show is that the higher animals have centers in their brains that turn on _emotions_ (not merely actions), and other centers that oppose these emotions. (However, in an unnaturally aggressive monkey, the "anti-aggression" switch does not work, or is too feeble to resist the "aggression-producing" part.)

The compelling question emerges: do we humans have the same kind of switches? Is there a way of getting at the aggression switch in criminals? Can scientists switch on pleasure and even love in human beings? Professor Delgado's experiments are perhaps the antecedents of tests that will allow man to improve—or possibly debase—his existence.

Delgado's brain wave

Although brain surgery can alleviate suffering it is drastic treatment and sometimes has a
devastating effect on the patient. Professor Delgado's experiments could mean
that in future surgeons merely have to locate an "anti-suffering" center and stimulate it electrically.

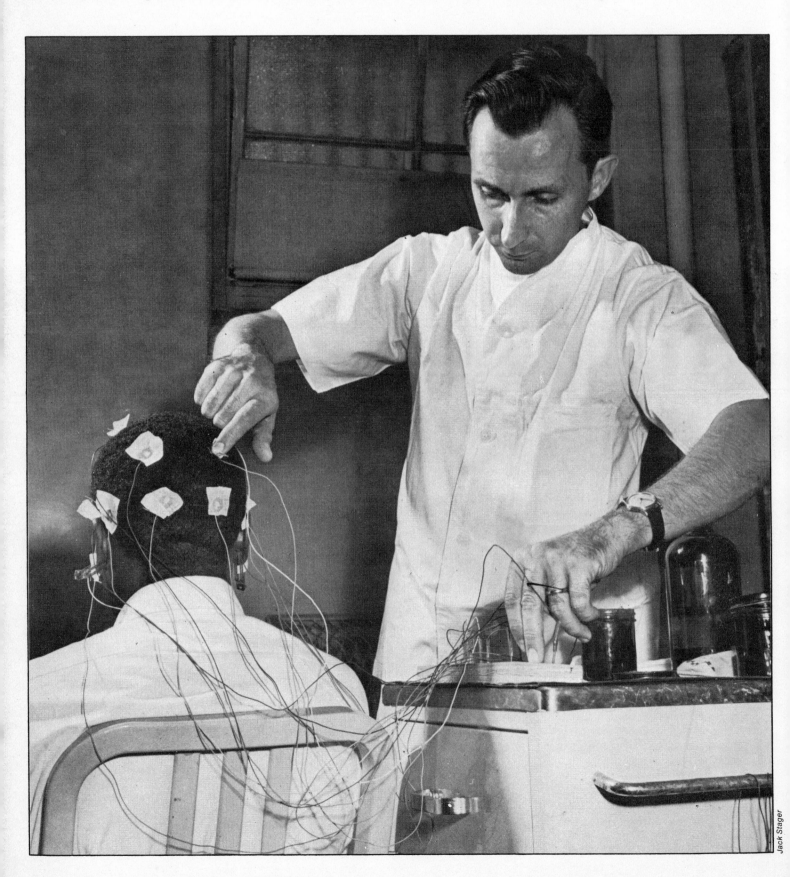

Jack Stager

If someone's heart is not functioning properly, he is said to have heart disease. The heart is then treated either with drugs or by surgery. Equally, if the lungs are not working properly, there is talk of lung disease. And again, drugs may be used in the treatment. But if the brain is malfunctioning, all too often the sufferer is merely talked to—in extreme cases he is thrown into prison.

This is putting it too simply. The ill in mental hospitals are given drugs that have an effect on their brains. One method of treatment uses electrical shock that seems to shake the brain out of its illness. And brain operations have been performed on some disturbed people to remove criminal impulses.

While treatment with drugs is helpful, the disadvantage is that the patient may need to take drugs for a very long time. This gives the body the burden of dealing with a strange chemical. As far as electrical shock treatment is concerned, no one has a very clear idea of why it works. And surgeons operating on the brain are destroying a part of it forever without being certain what they are doing.

Mysterious Epilepsy

If a heart valve does not work, it can be replaced. That is a logical repair. But brain surgery affects the entire personality. Some operations have cured the illness but left the patient incapable of thinking or planning ahead. In other words, the patient becomes barely human. Brain surgery like this is much too crude.

This is where Professor José Delgado's research comes in. At Madrid and Yale Universities he has studied animals that have had electrodes implanted in their brains. Now his research has been extended to human beings.

There is one striking advantage in using electrodes to treat people who are depressed or diseased or criminally insane. Put simply, even when the electrodes are in the brain, they do nothing unless they are switched on so they do not function all the time but can be regulated. They can be removed, leaving only a tiny scar under the hair as the relic of the treatment. And they are much more delicate than the usual brain surgery or drugs.

Epilepsy is a relatively common brain disease. During fits, the sufferer thrashes about and falls to the ground, foaming at the mouth. Eventually the fit passes and the person is normal again. The man or woman who is an epileptic may hurt himself during fits and cannot, for example, be left in charge of an automobile or any other kind of dangerous machinery. He also has to worry about when the next fit will occur and if he will hurt himself during it. And epileptics also have the embarrassment of having to warn the people that they work with that they may have a seizure.

As far as is known, epileptic fits are caused by some minor damage to the brain. Electrical "brain waves" recorded during a fit show that the regular patterns of waves are suddenly swamped by a strong surge of electricity. This surge starts from what scientists assume is the damaged part of the brain. So epilepsy could possibly be cured by surgery in the same way as appendicitis. First the part of the brain causing the seizure is found, it is decided whether or not it is irreplaceable, and, if not, it is removed.

Dr. Wilder Penfield, a Canadian surgeon, was the first to experiment in research along these lines. He opened the skull of a conscious patient, exposing the brain, and moved an electrode over the brain's surface. The patient was asked to say if he was experiencing the slightly odd sensation—called an "aura"—that comes just before an epileptic fit begins. This gave an indication of the area of the brain which was triggering off seizures.

But this method is a bit vague. The electrode is held against the brain with a firmness of contact liable to variation from second to second. Surgeons are very precise but might put the electrode in a slightly different place while repeating an observation. And even though a surgeon could bolster a patient's confidence, anyone would be a bit apprehensive about an operation which meant opening his skull.

Surgeons decided that they would rather use electrodes that were implanted in the brain. This method had a number of advantages. Doctors would know exactly where an electrode was located and careful testing could be done over a long period of time—some patients have carried electrodes in their brains for several years. And there was yet another advantage.

The brain works by a system of checks and balances, and certain parts stimulate activity while others inhibit it. An electrode in a part of the brain that checks activity could possibly control epileptic seizures. What is more, if a bit of the brain is "exercised," it seems to work more effi-

Dr. Wilder Penfield, whose electrode experiments on human guinea pigs have done much to reveal the nervous functions of the brain.

ciently. It is thought that it might be possible to "teach" the brain to shut off an epileptic fit before it gets properly started.

Professor Delgado has an even more striking idea. Nowadays, it is quite easy to put electrodes into the brain and connect them to a tiny radio transmitter embedded just below the skin of the scalp. It will transmit the brain's waves to a receiver in the same room or building. The radio set can be two-way, so that electrical impulses can be sent back into the brain. If the pattern of an oncoming seizure was recognized, a message could be sent out to control it.

But Delgado's most amazing idea goes one step further. The brain waves of the patient could be transmitted to a receiver linked to a computer. Then the *computer* could be instructed to recognize the waves that marked the beginning of a fit, and it could be told to reply with "anti-fit" transmissions to the brain of the patient.

In other words, the patient would live and move freely in his treatment

Philip Daly

Professor José Delgado, who through electrode experiments has discovered what appear to be the pain and pleasure centers of the brain.

room, and the treatment would be automatic. The doctor could supervise a dozen patients instead of having to devote himself exclusively to one. The system has not yet been tried on people, but it certainly works on monkeys. Professor Delgado has managed to restrain a particular brain pattern in Paddy, one of his chimpanzees.

After a week of two-way radio treatment using a computer, this pattern was produced only one-hundredth as often as it was at the beginning. If it had been the pattern of an epileptic fit, both patient and doctor would have been well satisfied.

In a totally different vein, something very odd indeed can be done with a pair of these two-way radio sets. Supposing one set was embedded in the skin of the skull of one person while a second set was put into the skull of another person and then both were tuned to the same wavelength. The brain waves of one person might then be transmitted *to the other person*. There would be real telepathy—direct communication between brains. This

can certainly be done, although it is risky as well as a bit nightmarish. But Professor Delgado is quick to point out that it is not telepathy in the way we usually think of it.

In "ordinary" telepathy, ideas and feelings are transmitted. Someone knows that his twin brother is in danger, or a woman "feels" a threat to her lover. But ideas and feeling and emotions, as they are felt by people, are represented by tiny, delicate patterns of electricity in the brain.

There is no way of detecting these patterns and no way of producing them artificially. And although it might eventually be possible to transmit the electric waves that correspond to a list of French verbs, say, directly to the brain, there is no chance of anything so like science fiction happening in the foreseeable future.

But even if a specific emotion cannot be transmitted—worry about a brother, for example—it might be possible to do something about harmful impulses. There are people who suffer an anxiety so intense that it paralyzes their life. There are those who are so aggressive that they are too dangerous to be allowed to move freely in society. And there are people with incurable pain that produces a suffering that is separate from the pain itself and more demoralizing. Can electrical stimulation of the brain help any of these?

There is hope for those who suffer because of pain. Quite simple surgery can cut down the suffering and dread without alleviating the pain—human beings need the ability to feel pain in order to survive. Unfortunately, the surgery may be simple, but it is still too drastic and it does harm to the personality of the patient, reducing him to a level below the truly human. Delgado's method means that surgeons will be able to locate an "anti-suffering" center in the future and stimulate it electrically.

Anxiety can be *produced* by this method. Professor Delgado has found parts of the brain that are related to anxiety. A patient with an electrode switched on in this area described the sensation this way: "It is something like the feeling of having just been missed by a car, leaping back to the curb and shuddering with fright."

Another patient felt that something horrible was going to happen and kept turning, looking around the room to see what threatened her. She felt this dread whenever the electrode was switched on. Unfortunately, no one has so far managed to prevent dread

by sending tiny electrical currents to the brain through electrodes.

Nor has anyone really found a way to check totally aggression in humans. The reverse however is all too easy. One patient, damaged by a brain infection, had moments of murderous rage. During those moments, she stabbed an acquaintance with a knife and she also thrust scissors into a nurse's heart. A record of her brain waves showed all sorts of irregular patterns, and one group gave a key to the violence.

Current Happenings

A carefully placed electrode could stimulate these destructive impulses. Once, the electrode was switched on while she was playing a guitar. She threw the guitar away and hammered on the wall in rage. This experiment showed where in the brain the rage had originated. But electrodes could not control the rage, and it eventually had to be diminished by brain surgery.

There seems to be something degrading about the idea that human fears and hopes or even rages can be produced by the electrical waves that Professor Delgado can conjure up with electrodes. But, looked at in one way, although personality is the result of distinctly human experience, that experience reaches the brain in the form of electrical currents passed along nerves.

It is wrong to say that the brain is "nothing but an electrical system" because that would mean that it should be something better. Nobody is upset by the idea that the heart is just a pump. And it is no more degrading to say that human feelings come from the interpretation of electrical currents.

As a result of this kind of research, there is one even less dignified possibility. One area of the brain seems to be a pleasure center. At least it certainly exists in the monkey and is probably also a part of the human brain. One person who had an electrode switched on in this area described the sensation as a "complete happiness." Another said it was like an endless build-up towards an orgasm. There is no telling what a person might be induced to do for such a reward.

In the wrong hands, this technique for governing pleasure and pain could be used to the detriment of society. It is not difficult to visualize a world in which electrodes could be implanted in the brains of all those who opposed the state or who were considered a social liability.

The honeymoon

A honeymoon should not merely be regarded as a few days' bliss in the sun. It should also be a time during which the newly married couple adjust to each other and learn to give and take.

Nearly every couple in the Western world who gets married goes away for a honeymoon, even if they were already living together before the wedding. It is a tradition as hallowed as white bridal gowns, orange blossom and the bachelor's last gay fling on the eve of the marriage.

The word "honeymoon" has been in common use in the English language since the sixteenth century in the sense in which we use it today. Dr. Johnson, not exactly the greatest romantic in history, defined it as "the first month after marriage when there is nothing but tenderness and pleasure." Most European languages use the identical expression—*Honigmond* in German, *lune de miel* in French, *luna di miele* in Italian and *luna de miel* in Spanish. Even the Greeks have a word for it although they prefer "honeymonth."

The actual derivation of the word is obscure. "Honey," of course, is sweet and, in the United States, a common term of endearment. Among primitive peoples it also has a symbolic significance. Many of them smear the pole of the newly wed couple's tent with honey shortly after the ceremony. This is supposed to ensure prosperity and, in particular, an abundance of basic foodstuffs in the, hopefully, long years of married life ahead.

Moonstruck

"Moon" has had a romantic association with lovers for centuries. It seems likely, however, that the actual combined word "honeymoon" was born out of a realistic—even jaundiced—view of marriage rather than a romantic one. The Oxford Dictionary, usually reliable in these matters, says in its matter-of-fact way: "Originally having no reference to the period of a month, but comparing the mutual affection of newly married persons to the moon, which is no sooner full than it begins to wane."

In the more leisurely eighteenth and nineteenth centuries the honeymoon was quite commonly referred to—and still is in German (*Hochzeitzreise*) and French (*voyage de noces*)—as "the wedding journey." Young couples from the aristocracy and upper-middle

Pictorial Press

classes would set off on Grand Tours lasting six months or even longer.

The romantic novelist George Eliot once explained that the purpose of these extended journeys was "to isolate two people on the grounds that they are all the world to each other." Brides, however, tended, like the Oxford Dictionary, to adopt a more practical attitude to the matter and realized that, having been more or less insulated from men all their lives by the strict social rules of the age, to be locked up with one night and day for six months or longer was likely to prove a trying experience. If they could afford it they usually took their chief bridesmaid along on the honeymoon to provide a little feminine light relief. Maria, the heroine of Jane Austen's *Mansfield Park*, for example, took her sister with her, explaining bluntly that she could not be expected "to listen to a man's conversation *all* of the time."

In that formal era of visiting cards, chaperones, and afternoon tea dances where physical contact was largely restricted to a clasp of fingers, an age when courtships were largely conducted in public with, perhaps, an occasional stroll *a deux* in the rose garden, a honeymoon was virtually essential. It was the first genuine chance a couple had to get to know

each other, to find out what they thought about life, to let their hair down (figuratively and literally), to grapple with the taboo subject of sex. But how relevant is the honeymoon to our own more knowledgeable, more free-and-easy age?

Nowadays, of course, most couples know a great deal about each other before they marry. They have normally discussed such basic matters as money, how they are to set up home, children, birth control, in-laws. Even if they have not slept together they usually have some shared experience of day-to-day living by having gone away on a joint holiday. They know each other's likes and dislikes, the interests they share and the ones they do not.

Yet, even today, a honeymoon is a valuable and necessary experience. Sometimes couples decide not to marry until they have set up a home for themselves, and then, having put all their savings into carpets, curtains and furniture, decide a honeymoon would be a wasteful luxury. They move straight into their home and start living like an old married couple.

Mutual Adaptation

Most brides who have begun married life like this confess, on reflection, to a feeling of regret. "I thought I wouldn't miss the honeymoon," explained one, "but, when I woke up the next morning and had to get up and cook the breakfast, I had a sudden sense of loss. It seemed as if something was missing from the wedding, almost as if I hadn't been married at all."

The truth of the matter is that, no matter how long they have known each other and how well they know each other, a newly married couple is not an old married couple. In terms of all kinds of everyday matters, like curlers, being kissed by a man who has not shaved, washing out socks and leaving the cap off the toothpaste, they are, by and large, strangers to each other.

In the past, whenever they met, they tended to look their best and be at their best. If ever their emotional batteries needed recharging, they had the time and opportunity to recharge them—in private. Now they are going to be together 24 hours a day, warts and all. They will find things out about each other, explore facets of each other's character, that they never guessed at before.

One classic case is the puzzled bride who discovered an unexpected aspect of her new husband's character when they reached their honeymoon hotel. He refused to hire a porter to carry in their pile of suitcases and, instead, insisted on carrying them himself. "My God," she suddenly realized, "he's cheap."

Discoveries like this have to be made—and faced—away from family and friends, in some strange, and preferably romantic, place where there are just the two of you, where you are insulated from such day-to-day problems as the husband's relationship with his immediate boss and the new housewife trying to decide whether to stick to her tried and trusted fish pie or try the recipe for *coq au vin* in the cookery book someone gave her as a wedding present.

Honeymoon Heartbreak

Perhaps the best argument for the need, even today, for a honeymoon is that so many of them turn out to be a disappointment; there is a lot to be learned from this lesson. The isolation of "two people who are all the world to each other," the time after marriage "when there is nothing but tenderness and pleasure," rarely turns out to be the golden memory a couple will treasure all their lives. Sometimes, indeed, a honeymoon can prove not so much a disappointment as a disaster—emotionally, psychologically or physically, and sometimes all three.

One of the main problems, of course, is that couples go on honeymoon at the wrong time—immediately after the wedding. There is a very good case to be made for splitting up after the reception and spending a couple of days apart—in their own homes, perhaps—before setting out on their honeymoon voyage of discovery. The truth of the matter is that the business of getting married is an exhausting experience, and what the couple usually needs most is a good rest rather than having to face immediately the new challenge of "getting to know each other."

For the bride, if it has been a big wedding, there have been weeks of excitement and decisions, choosing clothes, settling the menu, picking bridesmaids, making up lists of guests, coping with last-minute crises. Then the wedding day itself—the hairdo, the dressing, the ceremony, standing to receive the guests at the reception; the emotional wrench of the final good-bye to parents and brothers and sisters, bringing home the fact that she is leaving her former life forever.

The Reluctant Groom

The groom, too, has his problems. If he has celebrated the end of his bachelorhood unwisely, he probably feels at the start of the day that he is suffering from a temporary form of death. Mingled with his joy as he stands at the altar or before the Justice of the Peace are likely to be some somber thoughts about the responsibilities, and particularly the financial responsibilities, he is about to assume—mortgages . . . children . . . school fees . . . can two *really* live as cheaply as one? Under the influence of thoughts like this, bridegrooms—and even bridegrooms deeply in love —have been known to ask themselves: "What have I done?"

It is hardly surprising, taking everything into account, that the first night of the marriage often turns out to be a big letdown, particularly if the couple are inexperienced. Apart from the tensions of the wedding day, they have probably faced an exhausting journey. Now, tired and tense and hardly in the right mood for it, they face another momentous emotional experience—sharing a bed for the first time.

Strictly speaking, the most sensible course of action in most cases would be to put the light out and go to sleep. But that is not what is expected on the first night of a honeymoon. And, after the stresses and strains of the wedding day, he wonders if he will be able to perform satisfactorily, she wonders if she will be able to respond satisfactorily—and, hardly surprisingly, the answer is frequently negative.

The situation can be complicated by the fact that both bride and groom bring to the first night of their marriage their own ideas of love, based on their individual backgrounds, as well as the inhibitions they have grown up with. In the case of virgin brides it is also common to encounter an instinctive, almost mystical, fear of defloration. This phenomenon is particularly pronounced in primitive societies. In some communities the family and guests even watch the first intercourse take place. Apart from the desire to see the blood that is proof of virginity, these voyeurish rituals are largely meant to take the seriousness and the fear out of the occasion.

Other societies favor other methods of reducing first night tension. They range from performing the marriage ceremony by proxy to stipulating that intercourse must not take place for an agreed time—sometimes a considerable period—after the actual wedding.

This is in direct contrast to our own society which expressly encourages sexual activity during the honeymoon. At the same time honeymoon couples would often do well to remember the abstemiousness of some primitive communities and, instead of forcing the issue on the first night because that is "what everyone expects," they should wait until love-making happens spontaneously.

Even then, no bride—particularly an inexperienced one—should expect to "see stars" immediately. There is a technique to love-making as to so many other human activities. Because men are more easily aroused and more easily satisfied, the bride is the one most likely to be disappointed physically with the first night of her marriage. She should remember, however, that everything improves with practice and as tension and strangeness evaporate with the passing days. The most important thing is not to allow shyness or embarrassment to make her—or him, for that matter—clam up.

It is important in these early days for a couple to speak frankly to each other about their needs, fears and frustrations, not merely because this is part of what a honeymoon is all about, but because this establishes a pattern of willing communication and trust which will serve them in all the problems and difficulties they will have to face together.

Illusion is Delusion

Intimate physical adjustments are not the only ones that have to be initiated on a honeymoon. In the excitement of courtship, falling in love and getting married, the realities and responsibilities of marriage, the day-to-day demands of being a man and wife, tend to be relegated to the background. It is not uncommon for a bride or groom, and sometimes both of them, to wake on the first morning of their honeymoon, glance at the sleeping figure beside them, and suddenly think with a chill of what is almost apprehension: "My God, this is forever." This, too, is part of what a honeymoon is about—a chance to descend from romantic emotional heights and start thinking about mundane matters like the gas bills and dirty dishes that lie ahead.

Actually, the financial specter of what was involved in finding and building a home together has caused many a honeymoon in the past to be a physical disaster. Brides who planned to go on working and delay a family until they had a proper home and a bit of money put away found themselves inhibited by the fear: "Supposing I get pregnant. It will be years—maybe never—before we can afford our own home and give the children the kind of education we should like." Nowadays, with the greater availability and use of modern methods of contraception, that, at

Honeymoons are big business. There are now hotels catering solely for newlyweds. They will even supply photographers to take memorable snaps for the family album of the happy couple taking their first heart-shaped bath.

least, is one problem that has been erased from the honeymoon scene.

But another—surprisingly common and a source of instant dismay—still exists and is likely always to exist. Halfway through the honeymoon, sometimes much earlier, a couple are quite likely to find themselves sitting looking at each other with nothing to say. "Gosh," they think, "here we are, supposedly in love, on what everyone said would be the most magical holiday of our lives, and we're . . . well, bored stiff."

It is sometimes suggested that a couple who feel like this after only a few days together should not have married in the first place. This is by no means necessarily the case. They are not actually bored but victims of the change in their life style. In the past they saw each other for a few hours at a time and not necessarily every day. In between they led individual lives which sparked off plenty of topics of conversation when they came together again. But now, for the first

time, they are in each other's company constantly. Everything that has happened has happened to the two of them. They lack even the stimulus of the company of friends.

Awkward Silences

In the circumstances it is hardly surprising if, after a few days, they find they have "dried up." It is simply —and quite naturally—that they have not mastered the companionship of marriage, the happiness of just being together without the need for extraneous stimuli, without a feeling of awkwardness if they are not talking. They might take consolation—and instruction—from Jane Austen's heroine Maria when she, perhaps wisely, took her sister with her on her honeymoon to relieve the almost inevitable lull. Who, indeed, could be expected to listen to a man's conversation *all* of the time? Or, for that matter, a woman's?

A honeymoon should be looked upon, therefore, not so much as a few golden days or weeks of unbroken

Sunday Times

bliss—although you may be lucky—but as a time of experiment, of learning to give and take, of adjusting to someone you thought you knew intimately but who is likely to display some new facet of his character every day. That is why it is important to "go away" on honeymoon.

People usually behave in a less constrained fashion, more in accordance with their dreams and fantasies, when they are a long way from home and the watching eyes of relatives and friends. The new relationship has more of a chance to flower where everything else is new, strange, different. This change from the familiar scene precipitates a fresh confrontation between the two personalities; it helps them to forge the first realistic, as opposed to romantic, bonds between them.

Even for a couple living together before the wedding, going away together is still a valid exercise. They will, of course, already have made many adjustments in their personal relationship. Even so, living together and being married are not the same thing. Living together is a private matter: getting married is a public one. It is a social contract. The community bears witness to it. Although marriage is clearly an intimate matter between a man and a woman, it is also impossible to remove it from the social arena. As Briffault says in his book *The Mothers*: "The fuller our knowledge of relevant facts, the better we see on the one hand the dependence of the family upon the rest of the community and, on the other, the duty of each individual to contribute not only to his own household but to those of others as well."

The couple who, having lived together, decide to enter into the contract of marriage, have made a profound change in their lives. They are unlikely to encounter the physical problems of a couple who have

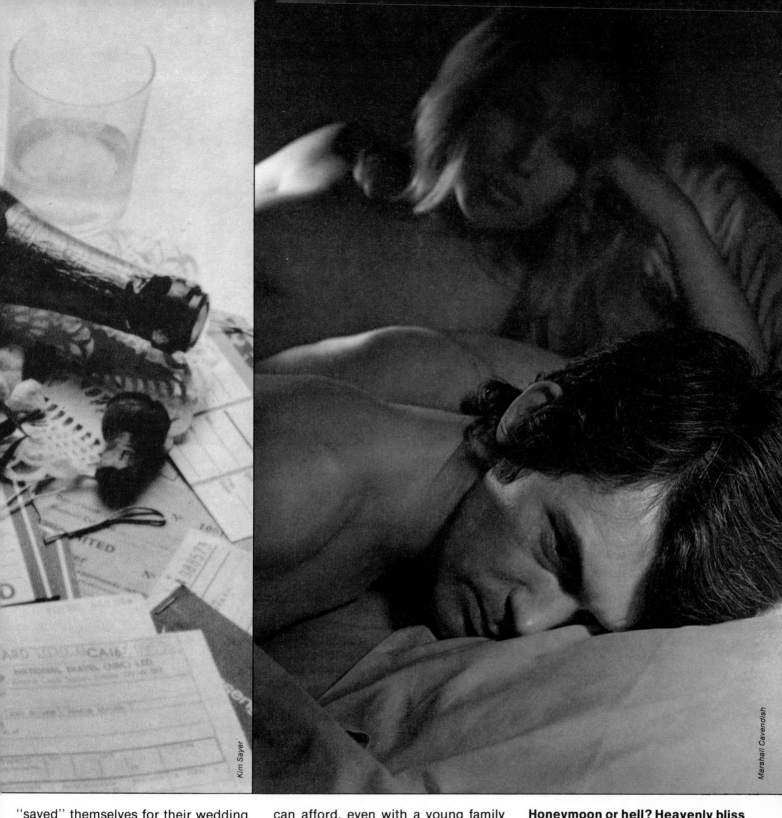

Kim Sayer.

Marshall Cavendish

"saved" themselves for their wedding night, but their new status involves psychological and emotional adjustments which, like those of other newlyweds, can best be made on a honeymoon, away from the familiar pressures of day-to-day existence.

For all but the rich, the honeymoon in earlier times represented the end of romance. It was regarded as a brief interlude when they could enjoy each other without cares. Immediately afterwards they had to knuckle down to the serious business of living—sometimes just surviving—and bearing and raising a family. In this more affluent age, however, most couples

can afford, even with a young family around them, to have a second, third or even fourth honeymoon. When middle-aged men and women go off on a second honeymoon it is not usually for physical reasons but because, if they have made a success of their marriage, they long for a little time alone together, to rediscover each other, away from the family and the mundane cares and routine of their lives.

Most couples occasionally need to get away together and recharge the batteries of their marriage, to sit back with no worries and try to recapture the days when their world

Honeymoon or hell? Heavenly bliss can shatter straight after the ceremony. Depleted by the wedding ordeal, newlyweds may arrive on holiday to find their partners are by no means as perfect as they had imagined.

was young and they were very much in love. Halcyon days they were, too. Oddly enough, no matter how difficult a time they may have had, that is how most couples who have made a success of marriage remember those honeymoon days when they began to change from lovers into partners, ready to face the challenge of life.

179

Pictorial Press

Portrait of The Boss

What kind of Boss do you work for? Is he aloof and impersonal, having little contact with his staff? Or is he avuncular and overly friendly? Perhaps he's fussy and neurotic or unable to make any decisions because he's in a constant state of crisis? But maybe you're a Boss yourself!

Your boss may not really be a Boss type—not everyone in authority is. And the true Boss may not be in an executive position, yet. But every real Boss, the kind that is either heading for the top at all costs or has already made it there, shares the same characteristics and drives. And if determination and sheer need have anything to do with reaching his position, he will succeed—or, literally, bust.

The Boss's personality is characterized primarily by a marked idealism and an overwhelming desire to succeed, even though he probably has his sights set on an illusory goal, a triumph that has no real value in terms of true fulfillment. His determination is often justified by the belief that he is bettering the human race or

adding to the wealth of nations, but his motivation is essentially personal and selfish.

This kind of rising executive is interested only in reaching his goal, and he looks upon the journey towards it as a waste of time. Anyone he meets on the way is regarded only for his nuisance or utilitarian value, an obstruction or a stepping stone.

The nineteenth-century writer Robert Louis Stevenson said that it is "better to travel hopefully than arrive"; this is the exact opposite of the Boss's style. Like the proverbial American tourist in Europe, he finds the actual trip gruelling but bravely trudges on—because it makes a good story when he gets home.

Because of his obsessive attach-

ment to this elusive goal, there is a certain remoteness and lack of warmth in the Boss. Human beings are relatively unimportant to him; so, while he has all the latest electronic communication gadgets—closed circuit TV and intercoms—they only serve to isolate him. And his actual relationships with people are characterized by an inability to communicate fully with them.

High Powered—Ivory Towered?

His aloofness grows as he achieves greater success; his office becomes an inner sanctum, accessible only after negotiating the obstacles of private secretaries, assistants, and outer offices. These are not necessary for efficiency but they are essential in

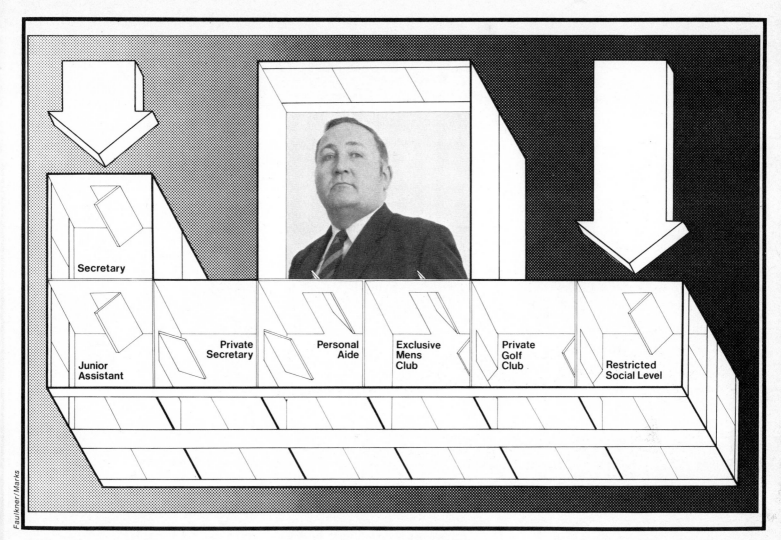

Faulkner/Marks

maintaining the Boss's psychological well-being. Similarly, his home becomes a place in the country, his telephone number taken from the directory. His luxuriously upholstered limousine embraces and protects him, and sets him apart. This tendency culminates in the obsessive isolation of a man like Howard Hughes.

At the same time, the Boss is not really cut off: he is apt to be a very gossipy individual. He knows all the latest office scandals, who is dating whom, who has just had an operation or a family row. Yet typically he may even institutionalize this tendency. It emerges in the growth of computerized information services and in the practice of many large companies who make it their business to obtain facts on the backgrounds of even the wives and children of their executives.

The Boss may sound like a fairly unsavory character, but there is one redeeming factor in his development, yet one associated with the disillusionment he experiences when he "arrives" and finds no satisfaction in success. His idealized goal was really, in business parlance, a "package deal": with success he should have achieved happiness, virility and the

Bosses often avoid mixing with their "inferiors." At work they are insulated from the employees by secretaries, junior assistants, and personal aides. Outside work splendid isolation is maintained by exclusive clubs, a large, expensive automobile and an out-of-town address.

key to what life is all about. Only when he reaches the top (but not until) is the Boss faced with the hard reality that his ideal does not exist, and this unpalatable truth may be precipitated by his children's recognition of his false values.

Coupled with his great affluence, this distressing discovery that the dedication of a lifetime has afforded him luxury, but neither contentment nor fulfillment, may propel the Boss into the world of culture.

This is the way that the great patrons of the arts are born and the priceless collections, Rockefeller and Ford Foundations and Guggenheim Fellowships established. And the long odyssey of the Boss finally bears the fruit of high social contribution and perhaps some unimagined personal satisfaction. This is the only other

avenue open to the Boss, and it is rare.

Culture and the arts are considered to be one step up from survival, a point beyond which the Boss usually does not progress. For his very survival as a personality is bound up in his pursuit of economic success. But why does he have such an obsession? A psychoanalyst would say that the whole Boss syndrome is a reaction against a feeling of insecurity and his obsession with financial success and security is a bulwark against self-doubt and outrageous fortune.

All of us suffer in some degree from a sense of insecurity, but the succeed-at-all-costs Boss has it in a greater degree. He attempts to buy security with success, at the expense—if necessary—of his staff and associates, family and friends.

The Sanity of Reality

By fixing his sights on such dizzy heights, the Boss can ignore the quagmires below, even though he might be quite practical and even ruthless in dealing with everyday threats. He does not live in an ivory tower; it is just that these threats have a different value for him as long as he trains his energies on his goal. They are merely annoyances along the route to what he is sure is fulfillment.

True emotional security is based on realistic goals, and recognition of this has been a big step forward in psychology. In the United States, Hartman calls this the "average expectable environment" and in Britain Winnicott tellingly speaks of the "good-enough mother," something the Boss is not content with.

Mother's Boy

What has mother to do with the Boss-type's intensity? Simply this: it is she who is the all-important influence in the early personality development of the child. The natural function of the mother is to make herself redundant, in due course to release the boy and let him identify with the father, as is normal.

But if, through a very early failure on her part, there is a lack of total commitment before the normal withdrawal occurs, the relationship is never quite adequate. And as a result, the child never acquires a sense of security sufficient to allow him to break completely the emotional dependence of that relationship.

Instead of his development progressing normally, he harks ever after for the maternal warmth and comfort which has eluded him. So, for the rest of his life, the character that is to become the Boss feels an emptiness and sense of desertion where there should have been security and affection.

This deprivation stems in part from what might be the mother's own personality difficulties (a lack of confidence in herself or perhaps a resentment of the child). Yet it may also arise from the mother's sincere intent of preparing her son for what she perceives as his future struggle for survival.

She wants her son to be strong enough to succeed in the outside world, modern business replacing the jungle. So she trains him through deprivation of any comfort that might prove weakening, little realizing that such early discipline will in fact make him hopelessly dependent in the most profound sense, though to others he might look vigorous, self-possessed and powerful.

The Battle of Waterloo might well have been won on the playing fields of Eton, but it was probably due less to the excellent training they received there than to the compensatory drives of boys born into families geared to packing them off to boarding school at age seven.

The obsession of the Boss may be disastrous for him, but it is good for progress. There is an inbuilt conflict of values between civilization and emotional health: civilization needs Bosses, and the mother in this case subconsciously, not intellectually, decides in its favor. In fact, society makes sure it will get the Bosses it needs by providing the right breeding ground. If insecurity and a threatened existence inspire the drive towards success, an unstable environment will prompt the mother to "toughen" her son, thus transferring the insecurity to him; secure environments will not have this effect (other personality factors of the mother aside). It is a question of cybernetics, of balance and control.

History bears witness to the cycle of growth and stagnation of civilizations, the younger, lean and hungry nations struggling and prospering, the comfortable, complacent ones degenerating. A look at periods of industrial invention and economic growth—as well as Olympic medals—supports this. They have been engineered by men with "drive."

But precisely since his position of power and wealth and the security it affords are so vital to him, so life-sustaining, the Boss is often limited in his effectiveness. He may not be a good administrator, because he cannot delegate authority or take advice but must make every decision on his own and control everything.

Jekyll and Hyde

And because the Boss dwells in a state of unrealistic euphoria, if disillusionment or failure ever overtake him, there is total breakdown and we see the other side of the coin. His counterfeit optimism and purposefulness shatter and he is engulfed by terror and helplessness. His emotional security has been dependent entirely on his economic security and cannot exist without it.

This tenuous balance is one of the reasons for the extraordinary vagaries of the Stock Market, so easily upset by a contagious loss of confidence. In fact, the entire Stock Market Crash of 1929 (and the incidence of falling bodies from upper-story windows) might be explained in terms of the sudden vision into the chasm by men who had never come to terms with it. Their loss of faith, once it began, was complete and devastating, and with this went the familiar panic and the collapse of the will to endure.

Economic reality is the only earthly thing the Boss really reckons with—

for him nothing else can compensate for the loving affection in which he unconsciously feels he should have basked in childhood; which should have been granted by a mother who, alas, exists only in his imagination, but who is real, for all that.

Certainly no woman of flesh and blood can replace her. The Boss's relationship with his wife therefore is always impaired to the extent to which his vital energies are directed towards his illusory goal. The idealized mother is a parasitic element in his personality, and his virility and capacity for human understanding are sapped by it.

All the Boss's relationships are characterized by the same aloofness he early experienced in his mother. But he can be a good boss, in the sense that he is not openly obnoxious, the more successful he becomes. His success imparts to him a certain confidence which gives him an aura and can make him actually quite affable, on the surface at least.

Father Figure

But like anything he touches, the Boss's own personality becomes institutionalized and he is viewed not so much as an individual as he is an authority figure. And the way his employees react to authority is how they will regard him—any shortcomings are on their part, because a symbol cannot be other than what it is.

In a relative absence of religion and of family hierarchy, he becomes the common conscience, and those who are most rebellious against childhood authority will get on worst with the Boss. From the point of view of the employee, it is his own personal difficulties which will tend to emerge.

But there is also a natural biological tendency for the young male to clash with the older male authority figure

Four different kinds of boss, from top. Dictatorial type: maintains an aloof and impersonal attitude, good at delegation but has little personal contact except through authorized channels. Clothes and large desk give no personal clues. Purpose of desk to insulate. Neurotic type: aims at perfection but fastidiousness leads to failure — see spilled ink and wastepaper. This boss will eventually make his staff neurotic. Paternal type: tweedy and avuncular. Staff turnover slow, promotion slow, pension scheme good. Insecure type: hang-dog look, constant crisis, cannot make decisions. Needs a good secretary. Recognize your own?

Ron Embleton

and to supplant him. Civilization covers this inherent conflict with the masks we all wear—we go about unbearded and unthreatening, conventionally polite—so the challenge is usually not expressed openly; it goes unrecognized and unpunished.

Success by Stealth

The one who benefits most from this duplicity is the emergent Boss, who bides his time and observes all the proprieties. He is amicable, respectful, even subservient, willingly suffering every difficulty on his journey up, because his mind is fixed firmly on the end, not the means. Thus it may seem that the meek inherit the earth, but the fervor and determination that lurk behind the mild facade of the rising young executive is what tells in the end.

In dealing with the Boss, as anyone who has instinctively survived deadly office politics can attest to, it is best to heed his pervading sense of insecurity, and to placate, to pose no challenge. Reprisal against any menace is as swift and fatal (career-wise at least) as a beast bent on self-preservation, for the quest for an ideal unthreatened existence is the very spring of his being.

The Cold Breath of Death

Little wonder then that when a Boss retires—or more disastrously, if he is fired—there is a nearly total personality disintegration. Typically he strives on until he is feeble with age, and death often follows closely upon retirement. Once he is robbed of even the faintest hope of attaining his illusory goal, he has, quite simply, lost his reason for living.

Petticoat Power

A woman boss can often be more effective than a man, for she has a greater capacity for delegating responsibility. This is one of the reasons 70 to 80 percent of all capital is in the hands of women; they have the ability to make—to *let*—other people work for them. Empires have traditionally grown under female monarchs like Elizabeth I, Catherine the Great, Victoria, and in modern times, Golda Meir. And cultural climates have flourished, because a woman can allow and sponsor the emergence of outstanding male figures.

She is very practical and realistic in delegating only to men with real qualities, for the more they achieve, the greater her renown; they in no way threaten her but only enhance her position.

Queen of the Hive

However, a woman can never delegate authority to another woman unless there is a lesbian attraction between them—there is room for just one queen bee!

It is because a woman boss is generally surrounded only by men that she has this capacity for indirect rule. Perhaps if men were surrounded only by female workers they would have the same ability.

But while a widow tends to enhance the growth of a financial empire rather than let it run down, she will usually have to inherit it rather than conquer it on her own. A woman is just as likely to have the same pathological identification with the inadequate mother, but for a variety of biological and social reasons, she may lack the sustained, focused, channeled energy, the single-minded drive towards success.

Universal Pictorial Press

B.P.C.

This is not to say she does not feel the same insecurity that propels a man, but it finds other outlets, usually transferring to her children. It could be that "Bossness," like hemophilia, is a malady transmitted by the mother and manifested in her son.

B.P.C.

Behind every great man there is a woman . . . Studies show women make good bosses because they find it easy to delegate responsibility. Women like Elizabeth I, Queen Victoria, and Golda Meir would seem to bear this out. Perhaps there is something in it after all!

All you want to know about…

psychotherapy

Paul de Saint Etienne d'après le tableau de VIERGE

Mary Evans

Q WHAT ARE THE MAIN SCHOOLS OF PSYCHO-THERAPY?

A It is hard to lay down definite rules about this, but many authorities believe that there are four dominating and successful approaches to *reconstructive* (as opposed to *supportive*) psychotherapy operating at present. These are Client-centered Therapy, based on the theories of Carl Rogers, Behavioral Psychotherapy, based originally on the theoretical approaches of B. F. Skinner and developed by Mowrer, Miller and others, Existential Psychology, pioneered by Laing and Cooper in Europe and Szasz in the United States, and Psychoanalysis and its many variants. It is hardly

fair to paraphrase the complexities and subtleties of these four approaches, but as a simple guide they can be summarized as follows:

1. *Client-centered Therapy:* This is a relatively recent development in which the role of the therapist tends to be notably passive, acting more as a sounding board for the patient's (significantly he is known as the ''client'') communications. The principal thesis is that personality restructuring should be done largely by the patient himself, who is led gently, with the minimum intervention from the therapist, to explore his own unconscious conflicts by talking about them and ''working them out'' verbally. This contrasts dramatically with the approach of, say, psychoanalysis where the patient is more directly guided by the analyst,

and even occasionally confronted by him with an interpretation or insight into his condition. Client-centered therapy is very strongly entrenched in the United States at the present time.

2. *Behavioral Psychotherapy:* This is based in its elements on the work on conditioned reflexes by the Russian Ivan Pavlov and subsequently modified into a comprehensive theory by B. F. Skinner. This theory argues that abnormal behavioral patterns have been learned because of a process of conditioning—the patient at some time in his life has found that the behavior patterns of which he is now complaining were successful for some reason in overcoming a conflict or problem. By automatic conditioning these responses become established

185

in the nervous system, and now rule his life whether he likes it or not. Therapy here consists of reconditioning, i.e. eliminating the old habit by attaching a different set of responses to the problem area. For example a spider phobia might be overcome by slowly but surely "acclimatizing" the individual to spiders by presenting them in association with a pleasant object or a reward of some kind. Behavioral psychotherapy is highly controversial at the moment, though there is some evidence that it can be successful in alleviating certain sexual problems.

3. *Existential Psychology:* This, the most modern and dramatic approach, is also at present the most controversial. It is based on the thesis that there is in fact no such thing as mental illness and that bizarre behavior patterns are the individual's dynamic assault on an otherwise overwhelming set of psychological problems. The role of the therapist here is not to prevent the apparently psychotic behavior but to *assist it through to its conclusion*, with the hope that the psychotic behavior will be spent and relief will follow. The process is known as "living through" the psychosis. Existential psychology has achieved wide publicity, but it has only minority support among psychologists.

4. *Psychoanalysis:* The oldest and most famous approach to the problem. In this sort of treatment, the individual with the help of the psychoanalyst explores his unconscious motives and conflicts in an attempt to understand the part they might play in his illness and so to restructure his approach to life.

HOW MUCH DOES PSYCHOTHERAPY COST?

In both Europe and America supportive psychotherapy can generally be obtained at a very low charge, or even no charge at all. Psychotherapy of a more prolonged and intensive kind is rarely free, however, unless it is administered as part of treatment for a hospitalized patient. Psychoanalysis, because it is never a brief course of treatment, tends to be the most expensive and thus is rarely if ever available under government health or insurance cover. Even so, a typical psychoanalytic course involving, say, weekly visits over a full year might nevertheless be less expensive than, for example, a course of elaborate dental treatment. Britain is one of the few nations offering free psychotherapy under a health scheme.

Unser Leben

Can people lose their phobias by having them presented in a reward situation? Behaviorists say yes.

HOW CAN YOU TELL WHETHER YOU NEED PSYCHOTHERAPY OR NOT?

For most people—the exception being individuals suffering from psychoses or severe mental disorders, many of whom tend to be unaware of the fact that they are in need of mental treatment—the answer to this question is: "When you really feel you need it." For example, a housewife with a young family, perhaps a wayward husband and, let us say, some financial difficulties may simply find that the problems posed by her environment appear to be beyond her capacity to cope with. Her inability to solve the problems puts her into a condition of stress and this leads to a number of symptoms, the most common of which is likely to be a feeling of general anxiety. These symptoms she can suppress or relieve by a number of means—she may become exceptionally aggressive towards her children, unresponsive to her husband; she may gain weight dramatically by compulsive overeating or she may turn to alcohol for relief. In due course even these strategies will not help, for of course the original stress-inducing problems have not been eliminated. If circumstances do not change, at some stage in the game she will realize that she needs psychotherapy and will seek assistance from her doctor. A tragedy of modern society is that large numbers of people either neglect or are not aware of the warning signals which serve to indicate that personal problems are expanding outside the scope of self-help. Increasing attention is being paid in Europe and America to informing people of these warning signs, and

campaigns—rather on the lines of those advising people how to detect the early stages of cancer—have been launched by mental health authorities. Here are some of the more common signs that conflicts are building up to the point where outside assistance is required. Remember however that *all* human beings suffer from some of these conditions on an *occasional* basis from time to time throughout their lives.

1. In a young or middle-aged person, any marked change in sleeping habits which persists for more than a few weeks. This may include difficulty in going to sleep, frequent waking in the night, or unusually early waking with difficulty in getting back to sleep. It is important to note that there is often a natural change in sleeping habits which comes with age, and in people over the age of 60 much less sleep is required. For such people early waking can often be looked upon as "normal."

2. Any persistent and marked increase in irritability and bad temper which appears to be "without cause." For most people this will be indicated by a deterioration in relationships with colleagues at work, or with repeated outbursts against wife, husband, children or other family members. Again note that we are not talking about *occasional* irritability, but of sustained bad temper—particularly when such behavior appears to be foreign to the normal personality.

3. Any very marked shift in eating habits—either in the form of excessive eating or, alternatively, serious loss of appetite. In such cases either obesity or the wasting condition, known as *anorexia nervosa*, may result.

4. Any very marked increase in consumption of alcohol or other drugs. If cigarette smoking doubles within a few months, or the intake of alcohol goes up substantially over roughly the same period, then these should be taken as serious warning signals. The same argument applies to any increase in requirement of tranquilizing or sleep inducing drugs.

5. Any sustained and severe changes in mood—for example a prevailing feeling of depression or gloom which has no identifiable cause. Once again it is important to remember that we are speaking here of prolonged and major changes in mood.

6. The onset of any severe phobic conditions—for example, a fear or terror of going into open places, into crowded rooms, of meeting large numbers of people, of traveling, etc. Such phobias are often symptoms of an underlying stressful condition which may require psychotherapy.

7. The acquisition of any obsessive or compulsive habit which seriously interferes with a normal life. Examples might include compulsive cleanliness which means that an inordinate amount of time has to be spent in washing hands, clothing, etc; the compeling need to go through a complex ritual before embarking on any course of action such as triple or quadruple checking of doors and windows in a house before going to sleep; obsessive preoccupation with the safety of a vehicle before setting out on a drive, etc.

8. Any notable and *prolonged* change in sex life. This may include, most commonly, impotence in men, frigidity in women or an unusual tendency towards promiscuity.

At the risk of being repetitive, it cannot be emphasized too strongly that the above check list refers not to occasional bouts of one or more of the eight warning signals but to dramatic or sustained manifestations of one or more of them. Incidentally, the above symptoms, while distressing and debilitating, often yield dramatically to simple psychotherapy.

SHOULD YOU EVER GO TO AN UNQUALIFIED PSYCHOTHERAPIST?

The fact that a person has a qualification, whether it be medical, psychological, psychoanalytic or whatever, does not in itself mean that he is necessarily a good therapist. It does however suggest that he has at least taken the trouble to acquaint himself with the great mass of knowledge which psychologists have been slowly accumulating about human personality for the past hundred years or so. It also suggests that he has been taught the basic skills of therapy, the pitfalls to avoid and the signs which denote blind alleys and false leads in the therapeutic relationship. While there may be some "unqualified" therapists who have some basic attributes which make them intrinsically successful in getting at the root of a problem in psychoneuroses, there is no real way of sorting out the genuine from the quack. The golden rule therefore when considering the delicate machinery of mental processes must clearly be to play safe and deal only with those professionally qualified, for even if they do not know everything that there is to know about the workings of the mind, they are at least aware of the limitations to their knowledge.

ARE THERE ANY STARTLING NEW DEVELOPMENTS IN PSYCHOTHERAPY?

Not really. There are many claims of startling new developments, but most psychologists look upon these with great skepticism when they first arise. When a new technique, a new drug, a new approach is first announced, there is frequently a rush of interest, out the evolution of psychotherapeutic methods is really a slow but steady progress, rather than of a series of sensational breakthroughs.

IS THERE SUCH A THING AS "DO-IT-YOURSELF" PSYCHOTHERAPY?

Not really, for individuals only resort to seeking psychotherapy when they find that they are no longer able themselves to tackle the problems which are troubling them. Psychotherapy, almost by definition, implies two-way interchange of information—the patient describing symptoms, the therapist interpreting them and by subsequent discussion attempting to identify their true origins. The essence of successful psychotherapy depends upon the patient gaining some insight which can rarely be achieved by "thinking through a problem on your own." According to the psychoanalytic theory of personality, mental and personal conflicts are often repressed or "disguised" by the unconscious mind, and therefore no amount of introspection will allow the conscious mind to sort them out. To this extent therefore "do-it-yourself" psychotherapy is really a contradiction in terms. This is not to say that there are no ways in which people can hope to quiet the turbulence in their own minds without resorting to professional outside help. Often, inner tensions build up about relatively minor conflicts—the sheer frustrations of keeping a job or a home, for example. If these tensions are not relieved, then the individual may be heading into a generalized neurotic state, but frequently great relief and a discharge of emotions ("catharsis" to use a term drawn from psychoanalysis) can be achieved simply by talking the problem over with a close friend or family member. The process of verbalizing in some way causes the problems, which have remained vague and diffuse in the mind, to be made concrete. The act of speaking about them (when they are essentially simple) allows the individual to gain insight and hence eliminate them. Merely thinking about them is not quite enough, for the es-

sence of the problem can be sidestepped in the mind. An alternative approach, and one which often gives considerable relief in mild conditions of stress and conflict, is writing the problems down in the form of a diary or a daily log. Such tactics only work however when the stresses and conflicts are mild and the roots of the problems easily identified.

WHAT IS THE FUTURE OF PSYCHOTHERAPY?

Psychologists are the first people to realize how little is known about the workings of the human mind and the many problems that can arise as a result of the stresses and strains of twentieth century life. The picture is one of a slow but steady advance in understanding, however, and with an increase in this understanding must come greater hopes for more effective psychotherapy. The problem here is that many of the developments in medical technology and research into new kinds of drugs have had their greatest effects in psychiatric medicine—the treatment of severely disturbed individuals who may be suffering from psychoses with an organic or physiological basis. Psychotherapy itself depends for its power upon the opening of effective communication lines between one human being and another, a verbal exchange which seeks to identify hidden stresses and conflicts, evaluate them and try to provide a rational and satisfactory solution which meshes with the realities of the individual's life. On the whole, wonder drugs and elaborate medical equipment and techniques are not applicable here. For this reason many experts believe that the most exciting and far-reaching developments in psychotherapy will come as the result of achieving a deeper understanding of the basis of human language and communication. All psychotherapists soon become aware that their patients' principal difficulties are often a function of their inability to verbalize and make explicit the problems, stresses, conflicts, and anxieties that plague their minds. No doubt this is due more to the inadequacy of our language and communication skills than to the fact that the problems are themselves essentially indescribable. It is for this reason that many psychotherapists look to the growing new science of psycholinguistics (the study of the psychology of language) for possible pointers to exciting developments in psychotherapy in the next decade.

Natural v. Supernatural

We all consider ourselves rational, thinking beings. But how many of us drop everything if we spill salt or see the new moon through glass? We are, in fact, highly irrational and our all too easily conquered minds are still confused between natural and supernatural phenomena.

Until quite recently—measured by mankind's life span—the assumption was that there were certain natural laws which God was able to break. So could the devil, or his appointed agents, demons and witches. When something happened apparently in defiance of the natural laws, it was attributed to their supernatural agency.

In time, however, more and more phenomena which had been regarded as supernatural—such as thunderbolts, the aurora borealis and eclipses —ceased to be regarded as acts of God. The belief began to grow that there were only natural laws, which could not be broken; that there was no God, no devil, and no witches; and that the supernatural was a myth, compounded of human fraud and human gullibility.

Mansell Collection

In order to accept this proposition, it was necessary to reclassify a great deal of history as legend. Every era, for example, has had its prophets, sibyls, seers and diviners, capable of describing what was happening many miles away or forecasting what was going to happen next week. Every era has had its miracles: saints whose blood liquefies on their name day; monks who levitate during Mass and float around the church, in full view of the congregation; medicine men who kill at a distance, by pointing a bone in the direction of the condemned man or making a dummy and sticking pins into it.

All these, and many more, had to be attributed to mythologizing, or hagiography, or fraud, or coincidence. Even the miracles of Jesus had to be explained away. Eminent churchmen

Man believes he can prophesy or influence the future in many ways— by reading tea leaves or Tarot cards and by making effigies.

Chris Barker

Camera Press

wrote articles to show that He had changed the water into wine by sleight of hand (with the best of intentions, so that the wedding party would not be spoiled). As for His walking on the water, that was a mere hallucination.

Materialism—the idea that there is no such thing as spirit, only matter—reached its peak just before World War I. After it, the tide began to turn. This was partly due to the discoveries of the physicists. They had been the most rigid in their devotion to the natural laws. Anything which did not fit in with them, Lord Kelvin, the physicist, declared, could be the result only of bad observation, "somewhat mixed up with the effects of wilful imposture, acting on an innocent, trusting mind."

Paranormal Investigations

However, with the advent of nuclear physics, it was found that nature herself was breaking the laws. It had been taken for granted, for example, that nothing could be in two places at once, or get from one place to another without moving the distance between the two. But atomic particles, the physicists were forced to admit, could be in two places at once, and could get from one place to another without moving the distance between the two. Scientific materialism collapsed because it was found there was in fact no such thing as "matter." Shortly before World War II, Sir James Jeans noted that it was generally agreed among physicists that "the stream of knowledge is heading towards a non-mechanical reality; the universe begins to look more like a great thought than a machine."

At the same time, research was proceeding into what had been dismissed as supernatural phenomena; and it has provided a mass of evidence that they existed. Since World War II, as a result, there has been a rapprochement between the physical and the psychical, both sides hoping that the research done by the other may have useful clues for them. And gradually, realization has spread through other branches of science that the study of the supernatural—or the paranormal, to give it the name used in respectable academic company—is desirable, and indeed very necessary. This is because the old, clear demarcation line between natural and supernatural, normal and paranormal, can no longer be drawn.

This has happened before in history. When the astronomer Kepler advanced the theory that the tides might be linked with the moon, it was rejected by Galileo as an "occult fancy." Galileo believed that attraction at such a distance was contrary to the laws of nature, but it was not long before the laws had to be changed to admit gravity.

A century after hypnotism had first been demonstrated, Lord Kelvin could still repudiate it as a "wretched superstition." But soon afterwards, following a protracted investigation by medical scientists, it had to be accepted. Such advances, however, were piecemeal. The line between the natural and the supernatural was simply shifted a little. Now the distinction is hopelessly blurred.

At this point a difficulty arises. In the past it has appeared safe to assume that science could ultimately establish what is or is not scientific by objective tests. But the physicists, again, have upset this assumption. At the atomic level, the physicist Heisenburg asserted that "the objective world no longer exists." By observing an electron, we change its behavior.

In the same way, although there have been hundreds of successful experiments demonstrating extrasensory perception—the capacity of human beings or animals to communicate by means other than the five senses, hearing, sight, sound, taste and touch—the human element continues to intervene making it impossible to provide consistent results. Nor is it yet known what forces are at work providing the means for such communication.

In the past, these limitations were used as excuses for refusing to investigate the field of the paranormal. But now it is coming to be recognized that such evasions are foolish. Scientists do not know how gravity works or how a magnet can defy the law of gravity; but they do not for that reason ignore it. Nor is the fact that certain phenomena are subjective and unrepeatable in test conditions a reason for denying their validity. We cannot induce love at first sight in a laboratory, but we do not deny that it can happen outside.

In any case, what is important is recognition of the influence of man's belief in such phenomena. Even the most rock-ribbed skeptic, secure in his conviction that there is no God, could hardly dispute that the belief in God has been one of the most important influences, for good and for evil, on the human race. The same is true of the belief in spirits, or even the belief in charms.

To this day, there are countless men and women who think they regulate their behavior rationally. But the same people would drop everything they were doing if they happened to spill salt or saw the new moon through glass. And they would go through some ritual which they hoped would prevent occult forces from punishing them for their inadvertent act. We are all irrational, and an essential part of the study of man is the study of his all too easily conquerable mind.

How, then, did the split between the natural and the supernatural come about in the first place?

A century ago the French psychologist Max Dessoir suggested an explanation. Most of us from time to time experience some prompting which appears to come from within, rather than through any of our five senses. We call it "the sixth sense."

The sixth sense, Dessoir argued, was originally the first. Primitive forms of life do not enjoy the assistance of any of the five senses. They move around, or collect food, by instinct. As the other senses developed, however, they began to replace instinct. Smell and sound, for example, began to guide the predator to its food, or its prey; and eventually sight provided the best guidance of all. The sixth sense remained, but fell largely into disuse, except in emergency.

With the advent of memory and reasoning power, the sixth sense became at times a positive disadvantage to man. In animals, it works directly on the nervous system, activating a whole set of reflexes which causes them to fly, or jump, or run, or "freeze." They do not pause to think what to do—their action is dictated to them.

Unheeded Signals

With man, the same applies. We jump if we are surprised . . . go rigid with terror . . . run away in a panic. But, in civilization, these reactions have come to be regarded as a nuisance, making us look foolish as we do when a toot from a motorist sends us leaping for the pavement. So, gradually, we have been phasing the sixth sense out.

Man has been censoring his instinct's messages to his consciousness since he was able to reason. It was very necessary to do this if his new reasoning power was to be given the chance to develop. He had to find a way of selecting only those messages which were relevant to his needs at any given time.

But what the censor cannot do is stop the messages arriving. They lodge in the unconscious memory so firmly that, under hypnosis, it is possible to get subjects to recall sights they have never been aware of seeing, and sounds which they did not realize they had heard.

The consequence has been a division of man's mind into two compartments, and this has had repercussions from which we still suffer—for reasons which Dr. A. T. W. Simeons described in *Man's Presumptuous Brain.*

When an alarm signal from instinct reaches the unconscious mind, Simeons explained, the nervous system tends to set the established reflexes in action. The heart beats faster, adrenalin is unleashed into the system and digestion stops as the body goes to action stations, ready to perform whatever task is required of it.

But if the censorship manages to prevent the transmission of the alarm signal through to consciousness—as most of the time it can—we are not aware why our minds and bodies are keyed up or tense. So we do nothing about it.

If it is only a false alarm, this does not matter. However, sometimes the alarm signal is being given by, say, frustration over our jobs, irritation with our families, or concern over finances. In such circumstances the alarm signals continue without attracting the conscious mind's attention and, eventually, we begin to suffer from emotional or physical disorders.

The Mind's Eye

Hypnosis, again, makes it possible to observe this process in experimental conditions. When a subject is in a hypnotic trance, it is possible to feed his mind with bogus alarm signals. It will react as if the alarm had been justified and will produce appropriate reflexes.

Conversely, the symptoms can be removed, providing the correct code can be found for switching off the alarm signals or removing the reason for them. But ordinarily we are unaware of the signal and attribute the symptoms to overwork or a roving germ.

The other consequence of the division of man's mind, and the censorship which denies us access to the unconscious part, has been the creation of hallucinations. Instinct operated originally through very simple impulses, indicating "food!" or "danger!" With the development of, and reliance on, sense organs, however, instinct refined the technique. The mind was given an imitation smell, or sound, or picture. Thus man today can see either through his eyes or through his mind's eye, as we do in dreams and visions when there is no actual sight. A parallel is the process by which a radio set converts waves into sound or a television set converts waves into pictures. Instinct is capable of producing a picture so vivid that we assume we are seeing it when, in fact, it is an hallucination.

The Power of the Mind

The sounds and pictures which primitive man received from instinct were probably at first on the lines of a charging buffalo or himself running away (danger), or a limpid pool or a vision of himself drinking (water). They were strictly in his mind's eye, however, and, once the development of speech made it possible to talk about these visions, and abstract them from the original situation, there came the assumption that there was another world, peopled by spirits.

They might be elemental forces, or animals, or people, but they were real, just as real as people on earth, and a great deal more powerful because they were not restricted by time and space. They were not necessarily hostile. On the contrary, they would ordinarily be well-disposed and their help and guidance very useful. Mind's eye visions and voices were nothing for primitive man to be alarmed about. He used them—as man still does today when he is able to tune into them—much as we would use a radio to get the news and weather forecast.

With the development of religion, however, it came to be believed that such voices and visions could be, and often were, the work of the devil . . . as Joan of Arc found at the cost of her life. And the development of materialism, which followed, led to the even more unwarranted assumption that they did not exist; they were all in the imagination, or invented for purposes of fraud.

Even when, towards the end of the last century, anthropologists found that primitive communities all over the world took second sight, and second sound, for granted, the implications were ignored. When research into the trance state, through hypnosis, did eventually lead to a grudging admission that voices and visions could exist, they were attributed to hysteria, or to mania, and treated as psychiatric disorders.

So they often are to this day. In *The Ordeal of Gilbert Pinfold*, Evelyn Waugh gave what was, in fact, his own case history, though it was presented as a novel, of the time when he was taking a cruise on a liner and began to hear mysterious voices. The voices seemed to be talking about him and to him, mocking him, and generally making his life a misery. His evident assumption was that he was being driven insane—which in a sense he was, not by the voices, but by his inability to come to terms with himself. There have been numerous cases reported in recent years of people, often children, who have seen visions and heard voices, but have kept quiet about them for fear of being "put away."

There is every reason to believe that, if we could recognize that such phenomena are perfectly natural and potentially a means of enlarging our experience, they could be extremely useful. As things are, they are exploited chiefly by spiritualist mediums. But they are coming to be increasingly used in research into the mind's capacities, which appear to be vastly greater than we have realized—as the Cambridge psychologist Frederick Myers forecast a century ago. He expressed the belief that the unconscious would turn out to be a goldmine as well as a rubbish heap.

So it is proving. And among the "occult fancies" which are now being reexamined are many phenomena which, though still in the paranormal category, are gradually acquiring scientific respectability. What used to be the no-man's land between the natural and the supernatural has recently been mapped in Lyall Watson's *Supernature*, a book which reveals both the extent and the importance of research to man.

The richest field for new discoveries, the innovative modern philosopher William James once remarked, lay not just in science, but in "the old un-

Some of the strange and striking Tarot cards, which have been used for centuries as a form of communication by occultists. The cards are a tangible system for symbolizing the subtle and deep spiritual truths of God, man and the universe. They act as stimuli to the imagination and it is for each student of the Tarot to interpret them for himself. Different packs use varying designs and symbols, but there is a rough general similarity. Gypsies are believed to hold the original set of the cards and the secret of its meaning. There are four suits of 14 cards—Wands, Cups, Swords and Pentacles—and 22 extra cards called trumps or Major Arcana. Tarot cards can be used to tell fortunes, but occultists regard this as their lowest use.

classified residuum'' which lay neglected just outside science's self-imposed boundaries. Scientists, rather than confess their ignorance, either dismissed the boundaries or pretended they were not there. Now they cannot do so.

If the exploration of man's unconscious faculties, and of his instinct, should confirm the already abundant evidence that he enjoys many extra-sensory perceptions, it will not simply mean that the scientific textbooks have to be rewritten. Much of history will have to be rewritten too. Or perhaps it would be fairer to say that our attitude to what has been written will have to change.

We are unlikely ever to know if the witch of Endor really did conjure up the spirit of Samuel to forecast the death of Saul and the destruction of his army, or whether the prophet Elisha really could report, for the benefit of the Israelites, what was happening in the Syrian camp many miles away. The same applies to whether the soothsayer really did or did not know that the Ides of March would be fatal for Caesar, or whether the hundreds of people who were present on the numerous occasions when St. Joseph of Cupertino levitated really saw him flying around in the air over their heads.

But at least we will not be able so arrogantly to dismiss such legends as fairy tales.

THE MAGICIAN.

THE FOOL.

Tarot Production Inc.

Kim Sayer

Freedom in marriage

It is no longer considered necessary that a young woman should automatically give up her job when she gets married. Changing—and more enlightened—attitudes towards marriage and the role each of the partners has to play means that the couple can go their separate ways every morning—secure in the knowledge it will help, not harm, the relationship.

Everyone who gets married gives up what most of the world recognizes as a desirable and basic right—personal freedom.

In some respects the burden of loss falls equally on both of them. The man, for instance, gives up all other women; the woman gives up all other men. Neither is at liberty any longer to do what they want to do with their leisure time. The man commits himself financially for the rest of his life unless the marriage breaks up and his wife finds someone else to support her. The woman either immediately, or, more usually, when children come along, gives up her job and becomes financially as well as emotionally dependent upon her husband.

These sacrifices of freedom are made gladly in the first flush of romantic passion. This is particularly true in the case of the woman. Marriage is so important to her socially that the compensations far outweigh the immediate losses. These compensations are, in fact, so desirable that she may deliberately "trap" a man into marriage, using sexual promise to achieve her ends.

This is the traditional view of the marriage relationship which, in Western society, owes its inspiration largely to the Church. Now a large number of people no longer recognize the Church's authority. Similarly, parents no longer exercise the control they once did. In our substantially "mobile" society, young men and women, often still in their teens, not only leave home to live lives of their own but often reject their parents' life

style as a part of this change.

At the same time, advances in contraceptive methods and the readiness with which birth control advice is available even to the unmarried · are enabling couples to enjoy sexual relationships without the risk of bringing unwanted children into the world.

Sex Change

The decline of conservative authority and the availability of modern birth control methods has led to fundamental changes in the attitudes of many young men and women to sex and marriage.

Not all of them have been for the good. There has been an increase, for instance, in irresponsible sexual behavior: promiscuity, inexcusable unwanted pregnancies, sexual betrayal of stable relationships and so on. There has also been a definite concomitant increase in the spread of sexual diseases, a problem which calls for positive action.

But the same period has also seen a substantial growth in responsible sexual freedom, couples enjoying stable, caring relationships in which the woman seeks neither the protection of the legal contract which makes her into a wife, nor the traditional right of a mistress to be "kept." Whether or not the couple actually live together, the woman is almost invariably earning her own living and would not consider giving up her job unless the man is rich—and then, probably, only if her own job is a routine one.

The Marrying Kind

Yet, this growth in responsible sexual freedom aside, marriage is still the way of life that most couples choose. The majority, even when they do not want to have children, still seem to feel a compulsion to bind themselves legally despite commonly heard protests about the lack of meaning in marriage and the inevitable losses of freedom which follow.

When today's "mobile" man can achieve gladly-given sexual relations with his "mobile" woman without giving up his freedom, why does he marry?

It is almost certainly not instinct. Marriage is a culturally-devised system, not an instinctive one. The sexual drive is so powerful that most societies have tried to create equally powerful rules to bind a mating couple together in order that children of the union will survive and flourish in a secure, protected environment.

From the woman's point of view, these strict rules have eroded in modern Western society to that point that, if she feels attracted to a man, she no longer has to entangle him with the strongest bonds of the society in which they live before mating. She can live openly with him without offending against the progeny-protective reasons behind our marriage laws.

Yet, like men, the majority plump for marriage and the loss of personal freedom rather than what society used to call—and still does to some extent—"living in sin."

The reason is that society still exerts strong pressure on young couples to conform to the conventional standards of the past. Illegitimacy, for instance, still bears a strong stigma, and the most obvious

and immediate reason for marrying is still, probably, an unplanned pregnancy.

Apart from this, pressures from the families of either the man or the woman, urging them to conform, are likely to be the next most powerful force. The conventional parents of a grown-up son or daughter—and by the time their children have grown up most parents *are* conventional with their own rebellious days conveniently forgotten—are likely to feel relief that he or she has "settled down."

With a daughter they also enjoy the knowledge that she has achieved

THE
ENGLISH
House-Wife,

CONTAINING

The inward and outward Vertues
which ought to be in a Compleat Woman.

As her skill in *Physick*, *Chirurgery*, *Cookery*, *Extraction* of *Oyls*, *Banqueting stuff*, *Ordering of great Feasts*, *Preserving of all sort of Wines*, *conceited Secrets*, *Distillations*, *Perfums*, *Ordering of Wool*, *Hemp*, *Flax* : Making *Cloath* and *Dying*; The knowledge of *Dayries* : Office of *Malting* ; of *Oats*, their excellent uses in Families : Of *Brewing*, *Baking*, and all other things belonging to an Houshold.

A Work generally approved, and now the Ninth time much Augmented, Purged, and made most profitable and necessary for all men, and the general good of this NATION.

By *G. Markham.*

LONDON,
Printed for *Hannah Sawbridge*, at the Sign of the *Bible* on *Ludgate-Hill.* 1683.

Reading University

The complete seventeenth century woman, as this handbill shows, was a good housewife and little else.

the respected status of a married woman. The marriage, in addition, brings such parents a new status of their own, something to boast about to friends and neighbors. It is not at all the same as having to "admit" that their son or daughter is "living with someone."

Parental Pressure

Parents are also likely to cherish the *celebration* of a marriage. Marriage is an occasion of great emotional commitment, the joyous agreement of two loving people to devote their lives to each other. For the parents of the bride and groom, a marriage is something momentous and hopeful as well as an affirmation of their own cherished values.

If a couple who have started to live

together do have a celebration party, it is unlikely to be a family party. It will, in effect, be an anti-family party.

"Joining the club" of married friends is also a powerful force in favor of marriage. An unattached woman over 25 usually becomes alarmed by the rapidly-narrowing choice of men available to her. And by the age of 30 she has been made to feel an awkward social unit.

Old Maid

Condemnation of the unmarried woman, or pity for her, is age-old. Some societies in the past devised extraordinary means for easing an unmarried woman's degrading status. Michael Banton, in his book *Roles*, refers to a fictitious marriage ritual in a part of Burgundy in France. An unmarried woman of 25 could go through a form of marriage with a man in which she took a vow never to have any other "husband." This is, in effect, a renunciation of marriage. But the "wedding" was performed with great ceremony and the pair were finally conducted to the nuptial chamber where the "husband for the day" pulled off the "bride's" bouquet of myrtle, threw it on the pillow, and then went off with his companions before retiring to bed in his own home. After that the "bride" acquired the status of a married woman, or, rather, a widow.

Banton also mentions a part of Hindu India where the parents of a spinster could avoid discredit by "marrying" her to a tree or fruit. She, too, was then reclassed as a widow. The Burgundian and Hindu spinsters, of course, lived in strictly-regulated, religion-controlled, long-established communities. One might expect today's Western woman to be different. In historical terms, however, the time in which women have earned their own living, and in which free relationships have been practicable, is negligible. There has been no time to adjust. Women expect to be dependent upon a man: men expect women to be dependent upon them.

A man, like a woman, is quite likely to be impelled towards marriage by the feeling, once most of his friends are married, that he is the odd man out. The perpetual sexual chase becomes a bore and, despite the frequently expressed envy of his men friends about his freedom, he, too, decides he would prefer to have the comfort of an established partner for social occasions and a regular something-to-do, somewhere-to-go in the evenings.

Marshall Cavendish

In addition to the pressures exerted by parents and the example of married friends, another strong influence towards marriage as opposed to just setting up house with someone is that, generally speaking, men do not like sharing women they feel strongly about (nor, of course, do women like sharing the special man in their life).

Even if the couple have started to live together the man is quite likely to begin to want to commit himself and may even start to fear the freedom that their casual obligation gives to the woman. He wants her to commit herself exclusively to him.

Child or Grandchild?

If he is living with such a woman, he probably discovers as well that the freedoms he retains are impracticable — unless he is unfeeling, in which case marriage bonds would not hold him either. His obligations are much the same as if they were legally married. There are, of course, certain differences. Both, for instance, have the

This couple face the choice of living together or getting married. Whatever they do, they should allow each other freedom of growth.

fundamental freedom, as long as they remain unmarried, to veto the production of a child. Both also have the acknowledged right to end the relationship whenever they wish to, without obligation.

But, in practice, particularly when a couple have lived together for several years, this is a frail freedom. Few women are strong enough to end such a relationship themselves unless a new man captures their affections, and the man who wants to end it knows how traumatic an experience this unforeseen and unexpected rejection can be for the woman.

Once a couple have decided to commit themselves to a conventional marriage they are likely to find, in fact, that restrictions on their liberty of action stem once again from parental pressure and the example of

friends rather than from their own personal relationship.

Parental pressure is often responsible, for example, for a married couple deciding to have a child when they have been uncertain about the matter or may even have made a firm decision to put parenthood off for some years. It is a rare parent who respects the couple's right to decide against having children. Furthermore, such pressure often coincides with a mixture of feelings in the couple.

Step Outside

They are anxious, perhaps, about their method of contraception, its efficacy or its possible side effects in prolonged use. They are anxious in case friends and relations believe that they are incapable of having a child. They wonder if they are missing out on something important by deciding against, or postponing, parenthood, and, in the end, they feel a wish to bend to the pressures and commit themselves, like everyone else, to raising a family of their own.

In contrast, in their personal relationship, the freedom issue is rarely an overt one between husband and wife. Extensive statistics and research findings collated by Jessie Bernard, an American sociologist of long standing, indicate that—contrary to popular belief—marriage is notably more comfortable for men than for women. The man's seemingly constricting financial commitment, in fact, gives him a sort of freedom— freedom *from* choice, the peace of knowing he must work steadily and that his course is set.

So, while there is probably a lot less freedom than we think in deciding to get married (despite contraception and modern views), there is also, for a man at least, probably a lot more freedom than we think once he is married. He has accredited forms of escape into his "man's world" of clubs and sport. Wives, generally speaking, acquiesce in this. It is even quite common in Latin countries for men to regain their sexual freedom once their own family is established and the children are starting to grow up. For sex they rely on one or more mistresses although the affairs are carried out with the utmost discretion, no shadow of scandal being allowed to fall on the home or diminish the status of the wife.

From the point of view of the woman, conditioned as she has been in the past to a dependent role, the freedom issue is rarely a pressing one. Whereas the man is likely to keep up many of his interests outside the home after marriage, the woman—especially if she has children—is likely to abandon hers under the demands of domesticity. It may be, of course, that, like many modern girls, she has been conditioned away from interest in anything but a "fill-in" job and a good time, followed by marriage. Either way the result is that development of her personality is virtually arrested.

The dangers of this, both in the early and later years of a marriage, are spotlighted by Nena and George O'Neill in their best-selling book *Open Marriage*, in which they stress the necessity for individual development of both husband and wife, and the need for each of them to encourage separate interests in the other as well as enjoying the shared ones.

A Thirty Year Stretch

"The closed marriage contract," they write, "specifies that the wife's place is in the home. Her horizons are inevitably limited by her relegation to domestic duties, and it is hardly surprising that she often fails to 'keep up' with her husband, that he simply outgrows her. She is merely a wife, but he is more than a husband, having an additional role in the outside world that usually presents him with far greater challenges and wider opportunities for growth than are available to his wife. So long as she accepts this imbalance in opportunity, the chances of establishing herself as her husband's equal will remain minimal: not only is her status less than his, but her development as a person is bound to lag further behind his.

". . . no wife in today's world can hope to grow in a manner commensurate with her husband unless she is involved in some kind of activity, beyond homemaking, that makes commensurate demands upon her and that offers her opportunities equal to his for personal growth.

"Some wives may *think* of homemaking as a professional career. But

S.C.A.

Some men and women are "locked in" by marriage. Each has a fixed image of the other's role and there is little freedom for either to develop as individuals. For the woman home becomes a prison. Divorce is often the only resort.

nobody else will ... Furthermore, even those demands that homemaking does make on a woman (and they grow less with every new electrical gadget) have a life-span plugged into the length of time it takes to rear children. With today's longevity, that means that the wife will have 30 long years to share with her husband *after* the children leave.

Feel Free

"How long will it take, when your only challenge is making new drapes, to become boring to your husband? Not very long at all, a fact to which the rising incidence of divorce after 20 years attests. Finally, the relegation of the wife to the ultra domestic role ... programs her for mediocrity and dulls her brain. With her senses thus dulled she may be able to delude herself into thinking that homemaking and motherhood are sufficient to make her a stimulating companion to her husband, but she won't delude her husband. He will more than likely have already found or be searching for a more exciting companion on the side. This may sound a harsh conclusion, but the divorce courts support it."

When English Christianity in the sixteenth and seventeenth centuries, and later the Romantics, began to base marriage on affection rather than on family or business, a hazardous course was begun. It is impossible to order a couple to feel affection for each other for the rest of their lives, yet we now account failure of affection sufficient cause for the legal dissolution of the marriage.

If the institution of marriage is to flourish, it seems that it is women—and the teachers of girls—who must make the larger adjustments. Wives must learn to grasp freedoms as well as allowing husbands theirs. If we can find a way to balance the freedom losses with individual personality growth and resulting companionship gains, we might yet be able to "order" life-long affection.

Freedom on the Pill

These two diagrams show how "the Pill," which has meant freedom from worry for so many women, prevents conception. A pea-sized gland located near the base of the brain controls the 28-day menstrual cycle. Known as the pituitary gland, it triggers off production of hormones.

The ovaries are always secreting small quantities of the hormone estrogen and the ova or eggs are gradually maturing (day 1). Then the pituitary sends FSH (follicle stimulating hormone) to the eggs to ripen them. The brain gland also increases the flow of estrogen, which prepares the womb lining for a fertilized egg.

Then the pituitary secretes LH (luteinizing hormone). LH makes sure that the ripe egg is ejected into the fallopian tube about day 14. The follicle or sac holding the egg is transformed into the corpus luteum, which releases the hormone progesterone. FSH and LH are cut off.

Estrogen neutralizes the mucus at the womb's neck, usually hostile to sperm. Progesterone makes the womb lining thicker and stronger. The egg, if unfertilized, disintegrates by day 28 and is discharged with the uterus lining.

The Pill, made up of synthetic estrogen and progesterone, blocks the pituitary's secretion of FSH and LH. This ensures that no egg comes to maturity. The woman takes the first pill on the fifth day of her cycle.

The Pill's estrogen content strengthens the womb's lining, but the progesterone has another effect. It changes the lining so that the egg will not implant if conception occurs. Progesterone also keeps the mucus at the womb's neck thick and hostile to sperm. The last pill is taken on day 25 of the cycle.

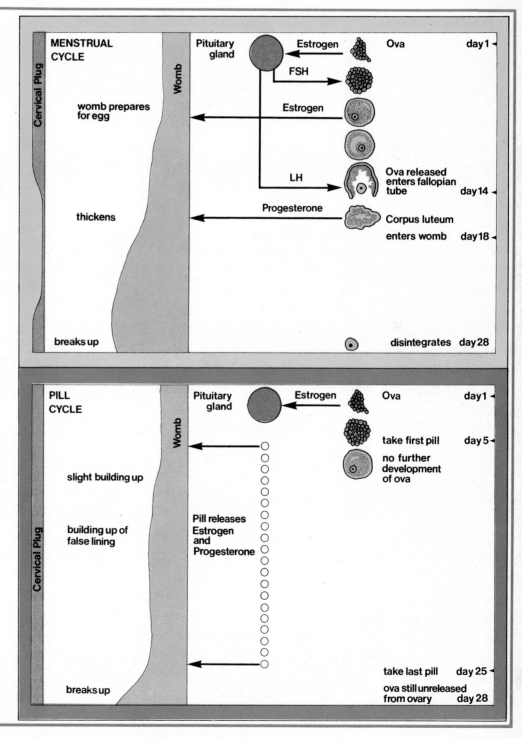

The jealous wife

All of us become jealous over something or somebody at one time or another. But the jealous wife, who thinks every woman is out to trap her husband, spends her whole life trying to protect her emotional insecurity. She is a very disturbed person, incapable of giving love herself but desperately wanting to be loved. Above all, she hates being ignored.

The jealous wife has one obsession. She believes that every other woman in the world wants to take her husband away from her. And, driven by this irrational belief, she watches her spouse's every reaction to a newcomer. Anything less than hatred and revulsion on his part will arouse and aggravate her jealousy.

This obsessive jealousy, a fear of shadows rather than threats of substance, is usually very obvious, even to a stranger. Another woman will sense it instantly. In meeting the jealous wife for the first time she will find a strong barrier erected against the proffered friendship. On introduction there is no open smile or show of interest in a new acquaintance, but a visible hardening of the eyes, a frozen social smile and a quick assessment of the newcomer's physical

A son talks with his parents as his wife sits petulantly on her own. A jealous woman needs constant praise to reassure her. She cannot bear to be ignored, and to be indifferent to her is to do her the greatest hurt.

attraction and charming graces.

If the newcomer is in the slightest way attractive, the jealous wife will instantly try to establish superiority in some way. She does not wonder if the newcomer is interested in her husband; she is sure she is.

Jealousy is something everyone feels from time to time. We each guard our territory, emotional as well as materialistic. Jealousy is born of fear, and few people are so secure in their relationships with others or their possession of some desired object that they do not, occasionally, fear an

aggressor who threatens them.

The woman who finds out her husband is having an affair with someone else is bound to be jealous, but the *obsessively* jealous wife is the woman who is jealous without cause. Luckily for everyone she is relatively rare. But when encountered, she can be dangerous and destructive to all around her, as well as being self-destructive.

A strange man will find the jealous wife a little less easy to categorize, but he will not be able to overlook her presence. She is preoccupied with her own appearance. She will wear clothes to show off her best physical attributes, and is almost always flirtatious. She will not bother to talk to another woman if she can talk to a man instead, and she uses her physical attraction to divert attention from her emotional and mental incapacity. Her manner will be a mixture of aloofness and seductiveness.

Mother-love, Mother-hate

Jealousy on this scale does not come suddenly into being, fully fledged. It is caused partly by the inborn primordial fears we bring with us from our animal past and partly by incidents and influences during childhood and adolescence. The jealous wife is likely to pass on her insecurity to a daughter who will, in turn, become a jealous wife.

Although we have spread our veneer of civilization over life, we still feel the basic fears that rule life in the animal kingdom and in primitive tribes. It is not uncommon in the animal world for a young female to oust an aging rival whose fertility is on the wane. Although the aging female will fight for her position, she knows that her replacement by a young, strong mate is inevitable. This is the way the continuation of the species is guaranteed. This is the system from which we sprung and which we all, in one aspect of our lives or another, fear.

It is a fear felt on the scale of generations. Each generation grows up eager to push its predecessor from power and then, in turn, fears the next

Living on her nerves, the wife who is jealous constantly has to telephone her husband at the office to check up on him (1). And she badgers him for gifts as tokens of love (2). But, at the same time, she needs to tempt other men, like the milkman (3), by revealing too much. And at parties (4) she flirts with other men. Certain that he has other women, she searches his pockets (5) for evidence to confirm her fears.

which will bring about its own downfall. When it is distilled to its pure essence within the subconscious of one individual, it can lead to the pathologically jealous wife.

The most significant relationship for the typical jealous wife is the one with her mother. In childhood there is an overwhelming need to split the parents, to take the father away from the mother. This is as much a need to attack the mother as to win the father's love. Every small child is dependent on its mother, but the emergent jealous-wife type has a hating-dependence because, in her subconscious, she knows the dependence is total. When others of her generation are growing up and developing into individuals, their mother-dependence is lessening, but hers never lessens. All dependence is a hating-dependence, and she may feel towards her mother rather like a heroin addict feels towards the drug.

So, to an outsider, this woman's relationship with her mother will look like an unusually close one. Her mother is her security and, although she hates the dependence subconsciously, she would never do anything to jeopardize security.

Because her entire security comes from mother-dependence, she will adopt attitudes which will please her mother, often accepting conformist opinions and becoming a compendium of all banal prejudices in order to stay in line. None of her beliefs will be held wholeheartedly because they are not held for their own sake. As a child, she is a little know-all because

she aligns herself with her mother against the outside world and to admit anything less than omniscience is to admit that she does not share in her mother's power.

The early wish to split the parents is a deep-rooted psychological desire to prove her existence, her place within the hierarchy of living things. She, like the rest of us, has come along as a replacement and her deepest urges are ruled by that simple truth of nature. When she flowers into womanhood, she fears those replacement urges in others, fears that, just as she wanted to replace her mother, so all others wish to replace her. Later, of course, if she has a daughter she sees the reality of her fears growing up beside her.

Although she, herself, lives with the fear that she did not marry for love or affection, she will present marriage in a very romantic light to her daughter and be ambitious for that daughter to make a good marriage (just as she probably made a good marriage to please *her* mother).

Unsure Allure

When the daughter achieves this, she steps out of the threatening role of the other woman within the matriarchal household and sets up a separate establishment in which the mother can take the role of "other woman." The mother will need to feel that she is attractive in some way to her son-in-law. The dangers in this are obvious. Primitive tribes in some parts of the world have laws which prohibit a mother-in-law ever seeing or speaking to her son-in-law. If she by chance meets him on some path near the village, she must step off the pathway and turn her back until he has gone.

Her image is all-important to the jealous wife's fight to preserve what she has. She makes the most of her appearance, often wearing clothes that are a little too revealing in her desperation to overshadow other females. She is the sort of woman who will not answer the door to the milk-

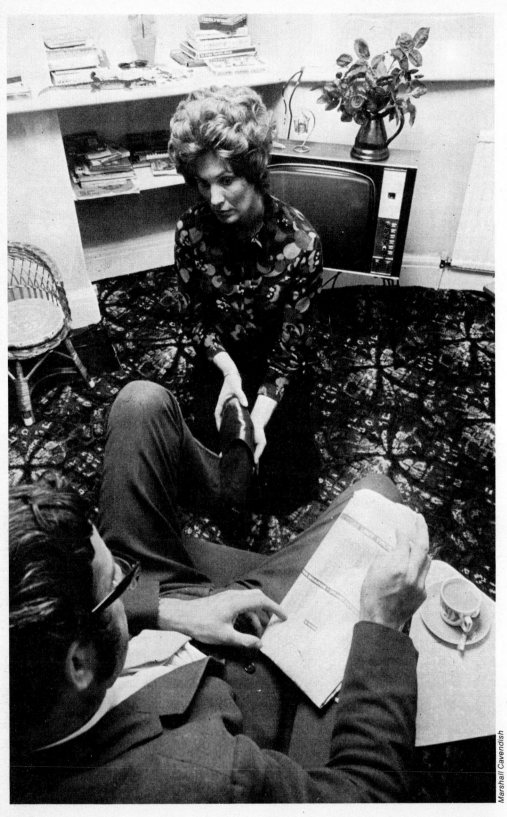
Marshall Cavendish

Obsessed by the idea that every other woman in the world is a threat to her marriage, the jealous wife can be overattentive to her mate, as is the woman at left putting slippers on her husband. Yet another tantrum may be just a moment away. The epitome of the jealous wife is the queen in the fairy tale *Snow White and the Seven Dwarfs*. She asks the mirror who is the fairest one of all. Learning it is the ever-present threat, a younger woman, she resorts to poison. And in the scene at right there is a tell-tale sign of the jealous wife who fears she is losing her charms—a book of exercises, lying open on her vanity table.

her self-esteem besides the constant attention to her personal attributes by the hairdresser and the beautician. She will be excessively houseproud and relentless in her acquisition of status symbols relevant to whatever society she mixes in. As her looks fade, the need for status symbols will grow and she is hardly ever at ease with anyone in case she lets the public image drop for a moment and so becomes vulnerable.

That moment of vulnerability would be worse than death for her, but it is inevitable. She is fighting her own mortality, which relegates her to the position of all other living things and regulates the simple cycle of birth, growing, maturity and death. She is, in fact, afraid of the harsh facts of existence—the system of fertility and propagation—which we all have to accept.

Tones that Tell

Having threatened her mother's fertility when still a child, she feels the threat from other women is one against her own fertility, and so she strikes back at her opponent in a similar vein. She would never understand it this way because it is a ghost from our primordial beginnings and not a logical specter from today's society. It is her fertility and therefore her part in the pattern of nature which she wants to protect.

When the jealous wife does reach the stage in life at which her fertility ends, she suffers a great deal. Death of the ovary means the death of herself. These women never have interests outside themselves which can compensate at this stage in their development, and so the rejection is complete. Culture will pass them by because to be cultural man must be above the survival level and have the time and security to forget for a while

man without her make-up on. This need for attraction becomes more difficult with age and so she will happily spend a fortune on cosmetics and rejuvenation treatment.

The Fairest of Them All

The jealous wife is the woman who shows herself rather than gives herself. Because of her dependent attachment to her mother, she is incapable of great attachment to anyone else. She has always put everything in

the store window, so to speak, and when her wares begin to fade, her worst emotional problems begin.

Fairy stories are often symbolic and peopled with true types rather than the hybrid personalities which most of us become. The epitome of the jealous wife, of course, is the queen who asks the mirror who is the fairest of all and, on learning that it is that ever-present threat, the younger woman, resorts to poison.

This woman needs other props to

Kim Sayer

the bare necessities of existence.

The jealous wife never gets beyond survival level. Her entire life is devoted to protecting her emotional insecurity, and so she will be interested in gossip because she needs to know what other people are up to in order to relate that knowledge to her own life, but she will not be interested in conversation about cultural matters which do not affect her personally. She does not really listen to the words people speak, but she is highly attuned to their tone, implying approval or disapproval of her. The inability to be creative in any way other than the building up of self-esteem leaves her an empty shell when she reaches the point at which that esteem has no basis to rest on.

Praise Her, Raise Her

In remaining at this biological level of development, the jealous woman is much less mature than a normal, well-balanced woman, and she does not have the ordinary person's values in relation to love and friendship. She is incapable of giving love herself but is dependent on receiving it. She needs constant praise, admiration and signs of affection. Knowing well the agonies of her own problems, she will delight in any signs of envy from other women. She cannot bear to be ignored, and to be indifferent to her is to do her the greatest hurt. Emotionally she is the equivalent of the Chinese girls with crippled feet.

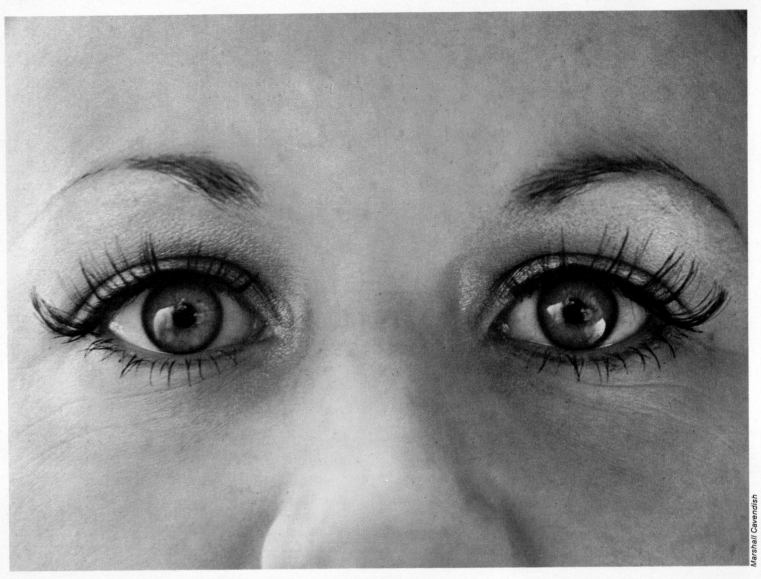

Excessive jealousy in men often means latent homosexuality, and in women it can be partly caused or aggravated by a latent lesbianism. Usually, when a woman looks at a pin-up picture she identifies with the woman in it, but an excessively jealous woman will look at the picture in the way a man does. Sexually, she is incapable of a true feminine role and, when making love, will often revert to fantasies. This does not mean she will believe herself capable of lesbianism.

Strangers Beware

Now how should one deal with this woman if one is unfortunate enough to meet her? The husband, of course, has the greatest problem, and, if he married her without realizing the extent of her jealousy, he is likely to leave her. This will destroy her and only an outsider will be able to see how she has wrought her own destruction. Any man constantly falsely accused of misbehaving is eventually going to go out and get what he is already paying for. Once this happens, the marriage is wrecked beyond

Jealousy is in the eyes of the beholder, especially in those of the chronically jealous wife. If her spouse shows interest in another woman, she is fearfully suspicious.

any hope of reestablishing it.

Usually the husband knows what sort of woman she is before marrying her, and he marries her because she is what he needs. She is almost always a good manager on the household side, and she is extremely ambitious for her husband so she will push him to where he wants to go. However, in accepting that he has married her by choice, life is not easy from then on. He must be constantly affectionate, especially in public (in fact, she would probably rather he were affectionate in public than in private). He must search for her good points and praise them as well as bolster her ego by pointing out *other people's* defects.

Her family has to put up with her, but strangers would be well advised to keep out of her way. For a man her constant need to be admired could lead to trouble. If he does not respond

to her flirtatious and provocative behavior, she is likely to seek her revenge by intensifying her efforts or starting ugly rumors about him. If he overresponds she will be incapable of keeping his advances secret and so, either way, he loses. If she is among the worst of her species, she will set her sights on the husbands of all her friends, both to assuage her need for adoration and to gain superiority over the other women.

A strange woman entering the world of the jealous wife needs to be on her guard immediately. She will probably begin by wondering if she has in some way offended the jealous wife because of the surprising degree of animosity. Once having realized precisely what the problem is, she ought to be as charming and admiring as possible, taking care not to mention anything about herself at all that might arouse envy, and then quietly slip away. There is no point in persevering in any attempt at friendship. The obsessively jealous wife is as incapable of true friendship with another woman as she is of truly loving a man.

All you want to know about...
SEXUAL BEHAVIOR

Q WHAT EXACTLY IS A "NORMAL" SEX LIFE?

A When people write and talk about sex, one of the favorite words you will hear used is "normal"—or its opposite, "abnormal." This is a great pity actually for there are few contexts in which these words have less clear-cut meanings. Sexual behavior is one of the most important forms of activity in which humans, and animals, indulge, and in terms of the survival of the species, or even of life on earth, it is *the* most important. Difficulties in defining "normal" are complicated by the fact that patterns of sexual behavior vary dramatically among animals, and there is even considerable variation in human sexual behavior. The question is also muddled by the fact that while the main theme of sexual activity is the propagation of the species—and hence all animals have strong drives to take part in it and get great pleasure from doing so—there are an enormous number of behavior patterns associated with sex, but not directly tied to reproduction itself. It might be simple if one could define as "normal" all sexual behaviour that ended up with the production of offspring. Unfortunately that would eliminate from the realm of "normal" all sexual behavior when birth control was being used, when the female was in a nonfertile state, after the time of the menopause, all forms of masturbation, all types of petting and kissing not followed by full sexual intercourse, etc. Once it is stipulated that sex *must* be associated with the reproduction of children, then the difficulties of defining "normality" are surmounted, but the realities of sex are then ignored. Probably the best way to define normality is to consider the patterns of behavior which are generally agreed by society. If a society, for example, feels that its coherence is threatened by—say—polygamy, and vigorously punishes its members for

Marshall Cavendish

indulging in it, then polygamy is "abnormal" within that society. In terms of his sex drive a man may very much want to marry several women at the same time, but his obligations to obey the laws of his society prevent him from doing so. Society's rules may change of course, and when they do the "abnormal" may gradually become the "normal" or vice versa. Western society, for example, is slowly changing its attitude to homosexuality and in most European countries, and parts of the United States, homosexual relationships between consenting adults are no longer considered to be antisocial. Individuals may of course strongly disapprove of homosexuality and may choose not to practice it themselves, but that is their option. If one was forced to define normality in this context therefore, one could say that it was *any* form of sexual behavior which did not violate the principles of the society in question. These of course vary from time to time and place to place, but it should be clear that even in the most repressive societies, leading a normal sex life would allow us to do much more than simply mate to make babies!

WHAT IS MEANT BY SEXUAL PERVERSION?

Again this has to be defined to some extent in social terms and one would say that a perversion was any form of sexual behavior which persistently violated the ethics and principles of the society of which one was a member. In most Western societies homosexual relationships, oral sex, masturbation, etc. are no longer considered to be perverse, though this was far from the case a century ago. The principal forms of sexual behavior which are generally viewed as "perverse" by present society are sadism, where sexual gratification cannot be obtained unless pain is inflicted on some other individual; masochism, in which gratification is not achieved unless pain is inflicted on oneself; pederasty, the desire to have sexual intercourse with children; and bestiality, the need to have sexual intercourse with animals. Of these four, bestiality and masochism may seem repellent or morally degrading to most people, but these are the principal grounds on which they are likely to be attacked. Sadism and pederasty, however, tend to be more rigidly prohibited by society because they frequently involve the infliction of pain or danger to other human beings against their will. Apart from this *social definition* of perversion there is also a definition in psychological terms. Many people seeking psychological treatment confess that their sexual desires have become channeled in directions which cause them anxiety or unhappiness. For example, a man may be sexually potent with prostitutes or with the wives of friends and yet not with his own wife. Or again, a wife may reject her husband when he most desires her, demand sex from him when he does not want it, and use her sexuality as a punishing instrument. In the strict sense of the word, such behavior is sexually perverse, and psychologists are aware of the fact that most people who find themselves in these sexual traps wish beyond all else to be free of them. The same pattern emerges in cases of homosexuality, fetishism, and so on. From a psychological point of view therefore, the definition of whether something is "perverse" is very much a matter of how the individual feels about it himself. If he is caught in any avenue of sexual behavior *against his will*, or can only relieve his sexual drive in a way that he finds worrying or troublesome, then he is suffering from sexual perversion.

IS IT POSSIBLE TO TREAT PEOPLE SUFFERING FROM SEXUAL PERVERSIONS?

If we accept that sexual perversion is defined in terms of either the way in which society views an individual's sexual behavior and/or the way in which an individual views his own sex life, then the answer is most definitely "Yes." Interestingly enough psychologists find that many people visiting them with worries about abnormalities in their own sex life or in that of their partner's are suffering more from ignorance than anything else. After one or two frank and intimate discussions the individual often comes to realize that what he has believed to be abnormal behavior is merely a normal manifestation of a rich and dynamic sex life. On the other hand often the problems are not so straightforward. For someone wishing to be cured of, say, homosexuality there is no rule of thumb solution. The therapist will first want to know whether the individual is seeking a cure because he believes that homosexuality is intrinsically bad or, for example, because it is preventing him from marrying and having children. For many people the best treatment is to show them how to adjust to their homosexuality, whereupon the guilt feelings which have been plaguing them will generally disappear. If however the individual is only sexually potent with members of his own sex and yet may passionately desire a traditional married and family life, then more thorough and involved psychological treatment is required. Such treatment, whether it involves homosexuality or any other forms of sexual behavior which are troublesome to the individual because they deviate from what *he himself wants*, generally involves a process of gradual reeducation. In all human beings sexual drives are, from birth, powerful but diffuse. In the course of growing up and maturing these drives become conditioned to particular patterns of behavior. Unfortunately at numerous critical points in one's life, these drives can be channeled into one or other of a variety of diversionary activities—the so-called "perver-

sions." Current approaches to therapy involve attempting to identify the critical situations in the individual's life at which the unwanted "diversion" took place. Once this has been pinned down an attempt is made to channel the diverted drive back into the main stream. It cannot be emphasized too strongly however that the use of phrases like "main stream" or "diversion" does not necessarily imply right or wrong in absolute terms. The real questions in sexual abnormalities and perversions involve assessing the behavior in relation to what society wants of the individual and what the individual wants of himself. No diagnosis, therapy or treatment is meaningful unless these questions are taken into account.

WHAT IS MASTURBATION?

Masturbation is any form of self-stimulation of the sexual organs leading to sexual arousal and generally ending in orgasm. It occurs casually in young children but with the onset of puberty, signaled by major developments in the genital organs and a great build-up of sex hormones in the body, it becomes a much more dynamic and consciously "indulged in" practice. It is enormously common among adolescent boys (George Bernard Shaw is reputed to have said that "99 percent of men have masturbated and the other 1 percent are liars") and is also common, though to a lesser extent, among girls.

IS MASTURBATION HARMFUL?

If no one did anything but masturbate then the human race would cease to exist. Fortunately while the practice is almost universally present in human beings and is observed in some form or another in many of the higher animals, its role is traditionally secondary to the complete sex act, and is most generally counted as a substitute for the genuine article. Taboos, more rigid in the nineteenth century than in any other time in recorded history, have surrounded the topic with guilt and anxiety, and it is still a common practice for parents to punish their children for casual masturbation. Punishment surrounding any form of sexual behavior, particularly when it involves children, is a psychologically disastrous practice, far more damaging and dangerous than any form of masturbation itself. Psychotherapists tend to find that many patients who visit them because of inadequate or tormented

sex lives are suffering from anxieties or conflicts due to guilt about masturbation, and many psychoanalysts believe that sadistic or masochistic tendencies in adults can often be traced to the fact that patients were painfully punished for masturbating when children. The majority of human beings tend to lose interest in masturbation when they acquire a satisfactory sexual partner, and it is here that a problem area can arise. In adolescence and young adulthood shy and introverted people often manage to avoid taking the plunge into an adult sexual relationship by a preoccupation with masturbation—conquests achieved only in the mind can be made without risking loss of self-esteem! If people are significantly inhibited from crossing the threshold of their adult sex life by masturbation, then to this limited extent it might be said to be harmful. Its value as an emotionally satisfying releaser of tensions which may build up from people deprived of the opportunity for a full sex life, however, enormously outweighs the disadvantages. Doubtless it also serves a safety valve function for people whose sex drive—for one reason or another—might otherwise become channeled into socially or even personally unacceptable patterns of behavior.

WHAT EXACTLY IS AN ORGASM?

An orgasm is the climax of a satisfactory sexual act and its characteristics are an abrupt "automatic" discharge of physiological and psychological tensions. Its major symptom in men is ejaculation of the semen and in women a series of contractions of the vagina. The intensity of the experience varies considerably from person to person and in a major orgasm, physiological changes take place in most parts of the body, and there may even be a brief loss of consciousness lasting for a few seconds. The physical characteristics leading up to orgasm are very similar for men and women but there is a curious difference between their capacity to achieve orgasm. For example, after ejaculation most men, unless they have been sexually deprived for a long period, are unlikely to be able to achieve another orgasm for at least 30 minutes after the first one. A woman, however, may achieve a second, a third and even multiple orgasms in fairly rapid succession. The duration of the orgasm also tends to be longer in women than in men. Sexual surveys of the Kinsey or

Masters and Johnson variety, however, show that on average men are more likely to experience orgasm than women and on a more regular basis. After orgasm body and mind become dramatically quietened and a sense of tranquility and relief from tension prevails.

WHAT ARE THE FACTORS THAT AFFECT AN ORGASM?

The principal causes of failure to achieve orgasm, apart from rather rare physical illnesses, are psychological. In the case of both men and women these psychological reasons are almost always either because one is not emotionally committed to one's sexual partner or the sex act, or because of some basic ignorance or inhibition about the sex act itself, or the nature of the orgasm. The latter reason is the one that prevails most frequently with women, though the matter is not quite so simple as that. A woman who is not really committed to the sex act may nevertheless participate in it, and be a moderate, if not sensational, partner for the man. Into this category fall prostitutes of all kinds, and bored wives and girl-friends. For a man, on the other hand, "passive" sex is literally impossible. Without some degree of commitment he will be unable to achieve erection and thus unable to insert his penis in the vagina. Most men, once they get as far as making entry, can achieve orgasm without too much difficulty. With women this is not by any means the case, but rather than make the assumption that this is basically due to some difference in a woman's inherent capacity to reach climax, the real difference could be dependent upon the different capacity to engage in passive sex. On the whole then, a man will not be able to even begin sexual intercourse unless he has a fighting chance of concluding it satisfactorily! Incidentally, occasional failures on the part of the man to achieve erection should not trouble anyone too much. When such problems become frequent and troublesome in either men or women we speak of impotence and frigidity.

CAN YOU HAVE SEX WITHOUT AN ORGASM?

The answer is "Yes," though of course it will not lead to full and complete satisfaction. The stimulation and foreplay which lead up to orgasm induce a state of physiological and psychological tension which is most efficiently relieved by orgasm—it takes rather a long time to wind down without this release. Women are somewhat more likely to be bothered by this than men, for just as the process of arousal is somewhat slower with them, so is the process of cooling off, particularly when they have not reached a climax. There is another fairly significant difference between male and female orgasmic capacity: whereas the capacity of a man to have an orgasm declines slightly from a peak period in his late teens until old age, there is no equivalent reduction in the woman's ability. In fact orgasmic ability may be at its peak in women in their 30s or even 40s. A reduction in this capacity—though not a very significant one—takes place with or soon after the menopause.

HOW CAN A MAN TELL IF A WOMAN HAS HAD AN ORGASM?

Perhaps the best way of telling, since orgasms vary considerably in intensity and in their external signs, is to ask her. This may not necessarily work, for most women know that men themselves get a kind of secondary gratification from the sex act by believing that they have raised the woman to the point of orgasm and her own satisfaction. This often leads women to acknowledge an orgasm whether it has occurred or not, and sometimes to simulate one in order to please their lover. One possible index is the erection of the nipples, which almost invariably occurs during love play. If erection has not taken place then neither has orgasm.

IN WHAT WAY IS HUMAN SEXUAL BEHAVIOR LIKE THE SEXUAL BEHAVIOR OF ANIMALS?

Man is himself an animal, and one of the great group of mammals called the primates. He shares a number of the essentials of sex behavior with most warm-blooded animals, in particular those which relate to the methods of reproduction—penetration of the female by the male, etc. However in one respect human beings differ very significantly from animals. This relates to the fact that men and women are capable of sexual arousal and mating on almost any occasion and at any time of the month or year. The exception to this is a mild tendency for a woman's sexual arousal to be greater just at either side of ovulation. While chimpanzees have menstrual cycles (of about five weeks), there is a definite peak of receptivity on the part of the female and the male, and mating is unlikely to take place outside this period. In other animals the period of estrus or "heat" is even more marked and is related to periodic changes in the release of hormones in the blood stream. How and why man has freed himself from biologically determined mating periods is a considerable mystery. There is some suggestion that the change may have come about when clothing or rudimentary garments were first worn and the physical signs of "heat" were covered, or when language was acquired, and the psychology of sex gradually became significantly more important in relation to its physiology. It is also possible that the acquisition of language and man's increasing consciousness of his own sexuality has led to the great variety of approaches to the sexual act—the considerable number of positions in love-making for example—which are not observed in any other animals. The acquisition of language and self-awareness of sexuality has led to some problems too!

WHAT IS AN APHRODISIAC?

Technically speaking it is anything which stimulates sexual interest and would therefore include sights, sounds and smells associated with the sex act. Most people however treat aphrodisiacs as exclusively referring to some kind of food, drink or drug and there is a very considerable and almost worldwide belief that certain substances when ingested will increase virility or sexual desire. The most popularly talked about (but rarely used) is the substance cantharides, which is extracted from the pulverized bodies of a tiny Mediterranean beetle—Spanish Fly. Taken in powder form, it causes severe irritation of the bladder and urethra, stimulating the sexual organs at the same time. Erection of the clitoris or penis follows without doubt, but the erection is often painful and will not be alleviated by sexual intercourse. It may also, if taken in too large a dose, lead to convulsions and death. The only other drugs which have aphrodisiacal qualities are alcohol and the illegal marijuana, both of which act by lowering inhibition and removing "social taboos" which the individual may have acquired about his sexual behavior. Large doses of both drugs, however, have the reverse effect, reducing sexual desire and potency. Some say the best aphrodisiac is the opposite sex.

John Webb

The witch doctor

The age-old authority and influence wielded by witch doctors, shamans or medicine men over primitive peoples derives largely from their apparent ability to foretell the future. Because of this, these tribal prophets are able to persuade their followers that they are indispensable. It is assumed that the words they speak come from the spirit world.

The earliest witch doctors probably owed their jobs to the fact that man was developing too rapidly, in evolutionary terms, for his own good. He was beginning to acquire the double-edged swords of awareness, memory, and reasoning power, and in order to exploit them to the full he had to evolve a built-in device to reduce the mass of information coming into his mind to manageable proportions; in the process, he lost touch with certain instincts which were very necessary for his survival.

For a long time, his reason must have been an unreliable source of guidance; and in that period it was useful for primitive tribes to have somebody who could go back, as it were, a stage in evolution. Either the

witch doctor could not have much in the way of an intellect, or he was able to cast it off, at will, by going into a trance state. There he could consult instinct, and inform the tribe what it was advising. Whoever could do this became a witch doctor, or medicine man, or shaman.

Spirit Worlds

When anthropologists began investigating shamanism, as it came to be called, towards the end of the last century, they tended to be under the impression that the witch doctor was a practitioner of witchcraft or sorcery or at least pretended to be. But this, they soon found, was not the case. On the contrary, his main function was to protect the tribe from the

baneful activities of witches, or from other occult forces which might do them harm.

He was able to do this not through any talent of his own—except the ability to go into a trance state. In that trance state, he either appeared "possessed," as if the information came through him from somebody else—believed to be a spirit; or his soul would leave his body for a while (that, at least, was his interpretation of what happened) and visit the spirit world. There, he would be kept informed about such diverse matters as where more game was to be found, what enemy tribes were doing, what witches were plotting, and how to cure some member of the tribe who had fallen sick. In other

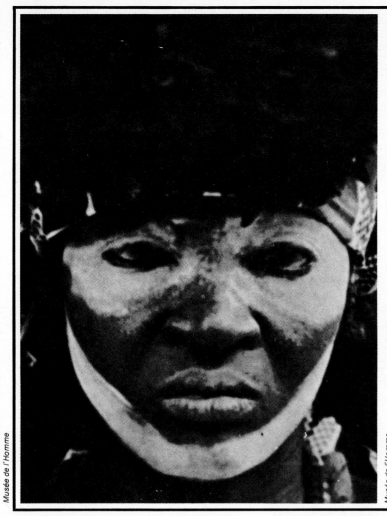

Musée de l'Homme

Musée de l'Homme

words, he was a diviner, a foreteller of future events.

In almost every part of the world, in almost every primitive community, the shaman, medicine man or witch doctor owed his post, and his influence, to this ability to divine what was happening, and what was about to happen. Often, anthropologists realized, divination in practice was little more than letting instinct have its say. But they also found innumerable examples of divination which could not be so explained, where the messages which the shaman passed could only be accounted for by some form of second sight, or precognition.

Since relatively few anthropologists have believed in the existence of extrasensory perception, they have been inclined to mistrust the evidence. And it is not, in any case, necessary to accept it, in order to understand the power of the shaman.

Sham or Shamism

He became powerful precisely because the advice he gave was not his advice; it came, the assumption was, from the spirits. It has often been reported that where a shaman is suspected of giving his own opinions, rather than those of the spirits, he is

The main function of the witch doctor or the shaman in the primitive society was to protect the tribe from witches or other occult forces, to cure the sick, and to foretell the future. After a frenzied ritual, they go into a trance which puts them in touch with the spirits. Above are two Congolese witch doctors and (right), clothed as a bird, a Tartar shaman of Russia prepares to contact the world of the dead.

soon detected and dismissed. Only so long as the spirits provided the information was it considered reliable.

In a sense, the shaman provided a curb on the chief's power, for ordinarily no action involving the tribe could be taken without consulting the shaman. The leader could not impose his will, or his whims, unchecked, because he ran the risk of calling down a rebuke from the spirit world. This was an important function for the development of society.

When the shaman was first under scrutiny, towards the end of the last century, his role was not properly understood, and he acquired an unfortunate reputation. Expecting to find that the shaman had been chosen for his wisdom, anthropolo-

Chris Barker

gists often found that he had been chosen because he was—in their frame of reference—a fool; sometimes actually insane. And so it must often have appeared.

His antics were indeed strange. To induce the required trance state, a shaman often had to make a very difficult and painful transition, involving what appeared to be an epileptic fit, with fearful convulsions. His information, too, might be transmitted in strange voices, like those heard during a spiritualist seance. To the casual observer it might sound meaningless babble. But the more remote it sounded from the shaman's own voice, the more it appeared to be that the spirits, not the shaman, were giving the advice.

A Nose for Trouble

Often the instructions were not verbalized at all. When he stayed among the Azande between the wars Edward Evans-Pritchard, later professor of anthropology at Oxford University, found that the witch doctors allowed their bodies as well as their mouths to be taken over. Instead of their performing a dance, it was as if the dance started performing them—controlling their movements in a way that would answer the questions the tribe wanted to know.

Evans-Pritchard's houseboy, who became a witch doctor, described what happened to him. Carried away by the rhythm, he explained, the dancer finds himself in front of somebody suspected of being a witch. If the man is not a witch, the dance whirls the witch doctor away in front of other suspects, until eventually "his heart shakes about him," and he knows he is confronting the real witch. The point is that the witch doctor exercises no control.

Even if the witch turns out to be a friend, or a member of his own family, the witch doctor can do nothing to stop himself from revealing the fact. And it is largely because he is so obviously controlled by outside forces that the witch doctor's authority comes to be accepted, overriding even the chief, because the chief ordinarily would never dare to offend the spirits—and if he did, he might lose his own authority with the tribe.

Other witch doctors have divined by "smell"—like Gagool, in Rider Haggard's *King Solomon's Mines*. The methods have varied greatly. But fundamentally shamanism is a "technique of ecstasy," as Professor Mircea Eliade puts it.

Colloquially the term "ecstasy" has become watered down. Eliade was using it in the old sense of a separation of the mind, or the spirit, from the physical being; a trance state in which the shaman's soul leaves his body and is free to roam to other regions of the earth, or the sky, or the

underworld, and to communicate with the spirits, and to collect whatever information may be of use to his tribe.

It may seem extraordinary that a subject of such great interest should have had to wait until 1951—the publication date of Eliade's *Shamanisme*—for the first attempt at a comprehensive survey. The reason is curious. The first real contact with shamanism was very early—when Columbus reached the New World and found the medicine man of Indian tribes. These were at first taken to be, and described as, priests. But the Spanish settlers soon found that they were not priests in the European sense, carrying out certain rituals based on a set of traditions. When the medicine man was asked a question he did not consult his memory, or involve tradition; he went into a trance and consulted the spirits.

The Spaniards did not doubt that this was what the medicine man was actually doing. Nor did they doubt that the information he brought back was correct, so far as it went. They were quite prepared to believe that, in his visions, he was capable of second sight, or of foretelling the future. What they could not believe was that the visions came from God. Why should God grant them to the heathen in America, and withhold them from his chosen people in Europe?

Case Dismissed

There could only be one answer, they felt; the visions came from the devil. The picture they presented was accurate, because if it was not, the medicine man would lose his power over the Indians. But the picture was also deliberately misleading—encouraging the Indians to torture their enemies, for example, after capture, as they delighted in doing. It was presumably the devil's delight, too. So the Spanish colonists called in the Inquisition; and wherever the inquisitors had the power, divination was suppressed, or driven underground.

As a result, shamanism received little serious scientific study until comparatively recent investigation; and by this time it had become suspect for a different reason. A battle was being waged between, on the one side, the orthodox scientists, who maintained that there were certain laws of nature which could not be broken—and who rejected clairvoyance, telepathy and the rest as superstition; and on the other side, the believers in mesmer-

ism, spiritualism, and other phenomena which scientists rejected as supernatural. It happened that one of their battle grounds concerned the trance state—ecstasy, as it was then described. Orthodox scientists simply refused to accept its existence; and when hypnotism was demonstrated to them, they dismissed it as fraud. They were equally incredulous about reports of the powers of witch doctors.

Hidden Arts

This put the anthropologists in a difficult position. They longed for academic recognition, hitherto denied to them on the ground that their information was no more reliable than "travelers' tales." But to get that recognition, they must keep their discipline free from any taint of occultism. Edward Tylor, who was to become the first professor of anthropology at Oxford University, could not bring himself to deny the existence of the trance state; but he was prepared to repudiate divination. So shamanism became divorced, in anthropological studies, from its main function—uncovering the secrets of the world. It was dismissed as a kind of tribal mania, a hysterical disorder which afflicted primitive peoples, leaving them prone to delusions.

A good example of this attitude was provided by Sir James Frazer, whose *The Golden Bough* was the first comparative study of primitive tribes to reach the general public. The notion that people might become "inspired" or "possessed," he asserted, had been used about abnormal mental states, with the result that more or less crazy people, particularly those suffering from hysteria and epilepsy, were "for that reason thought to be particularly favored by the spirits, and are therefore consulted as oracles, their wild and whirling words passing for revelations of a higher power, whether a god or a ghost."

It never crossed Frazer's mind that the wild and whirling words might contain any meaningful messages. On the contrary, he thought they represented a serious menace—"if the decisions of a whole community in matters of the gravest importance are left to turn on the wayward fancies, the whims and vagaries of the insane or the semi-insane, what are likely to be the consequences!"

It was not until anthropologists began to spend years in field work, living among and almost as part of the tribes they were studying, that they began to realize how mistaken this view had been.

Part of the credit for this change of attitude must go to Sigmund Freud. Freud's popularization of the idea that man has an active unconscious mind, containing a mass of information which only a form of censorship keeps from reaching consciousness, was a help in the understanding of the medicine man's trance state. Carl Jung made a more positive contribution with his suggestion that the unconscious mind contains material not only from the individual's memory, but also from some common source—the collective unconscious. And both men accepted that there is communication between minds by some means other than the five senses: through extrasensory perception.

As soon as it became possible to accept that extrasensory perception existed, the importance of the shaman became easier to understand. He was the man who, by his capacity to leave this world, could tune in to the broadcasts on another channel and from there provide information much more valuable to primitive tribes than their unformed collective reasoning power could give to guide their lives.

It could be argued, in fact, that in losing the shaman and his second sight, civilization has taken a backwards step. This, incidentally, is another reason why the Victorian anthropologists found it so hard to take shamanism seriously; they believed in the ascent of man from superstition to scientific rationalism.

Although the shaman-to-be may sometimes be mistaken for a madman, Eliade has explained, "in reality his 'madness' fulfills a mystic function. It reveals certain aspects of reality to him that are inaccessible to other mortals, and it is only after having experienced and entered into these hidden dimensions of reality that the 'madman' becomes a shaman." Once he is established, there may be no indication of eccentricity other than the manifestations of the trance state.

Tribesmen feared the power of the person who had been singled out as the witch doctor or shaman. Not only could he contact the spirits of the dead, he could perform magical feats and endure great pain. Acts like passing wooden arrows through the cheeks by witch doctors in the Congo were striking confirmation of their supernatural powers.

Life Line to Instinct

Much of the witch doctor's authority derives from his ability to convince the members of the tribe that he is indispensable on a very mundane level; "he is expected to act as a prophet, warning his clients of future misfortune, foretelling the outcome of a complicated venture, and answering any questions put to him"—such as how to find something which has been lost or, if it has been stolen, who was the thief.

Thanks to the work of Freud and Jung, it now seems likely that the keys to all existence do indeed lie in our unconscious. More and more "civilized man" is coming around to the point of view that shamanism has represented an essential stage in his own development, acting as a kind of life line to his instinct, when he was in danger of losing it.

Aesthetic judgment

"I may not know about Art, but I know what I like"—how often have you said that? Appreciating art seems to most of us a mysterious business, for a few specialists only. Yet Sir Herbert Read, the great British art historian and critic, said, "Art is most usually defined as an attempt to create pleasing forms." What *you* like is the basis of aesthetic judgments.

Look at the two pictures here. Study them for two or three minutes. Which do you prefer? Which would you rather look at day after day? Both show beautiful women; both were painted in the same century. But one is generally rated higher than the other. Manet's *Olympia* is an acknowledged masterpiece; Etty's saucy nude is fun, but not great art. Why? You may begin to answer this question yourself after considering a few basic principles.

Maybe you chose the picture of the woman who attracted you more. But paintings of beautiful people or things are not necessarily good paintings. Ugly people, or even arrangements of lines and shapes, well painted, have more "pleasing forms" than insipid pin-ups. The ideal of beauty has changed so much through different times and countries that it can give us only limited guidance.

One of the most important features in art is the creation of forms. Study the pictures of trees on the next page. They are not "Art" but show some of the features that make up art. The pictures are not quite identical; which one pleases you more? The right-hand picture is reckoned to be aesthetically superior. Incidentally, women on average respond better to this sort of problem than men, and intuitively pick out the "better" picture. What do you think makes the difference in the right-hand picture? Check off the list below:
MORE REALISTIC
BETTER QUALITY OF DRAWING
SHAPES BETTER BALANCED
PATTERNS OF STONES MORE
    INTERESTING
BETTER USE OF SHADE.
    Look again at the foreground of the

One of these pictures is fresh and imaginative, the other hackneyed and trite. Which is which? The subject does not really matter; nor does the prettiness of the women. What is vital is the way shapes and space are handled. You be the judge.

two pictures, the only part that is different. Can you see now that the drawing in the left becomes weak and poorly-defined? Compare the flowers at the lower left-hand corners. The stones on the left are monotonously regular, with very little shading, and the paths in each picture strike the eye quite differently—in the better picture, the eye has some interesting shapes and contrasts to follow, whereas in the poorer picture the same space is flat and dull.

The arrangement of rocks and path illustrates two of the most important principles of what makes "pleasing

forms"—*balance* and *surprise*. All human beings respond to pattern from the earliest weeks of life. Babies, as experimental psychologist Fantz discovered, spend longer looking at irregular patterns but return their gaze to regular ones. A completely symmetrical pattern of simple design begins to bore us quite soon; but so does a completely random arrangement. What we like to see is something which satisfies our need for harmony yet offers stimulating interest, appealing to a sense of order and a sense of novelty. These two principles run through all forms of art at

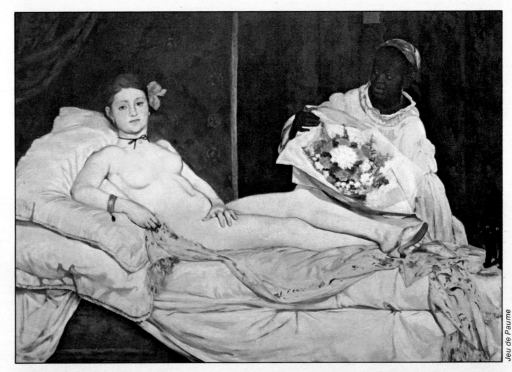

Jeu de Paume

Tate Gallery

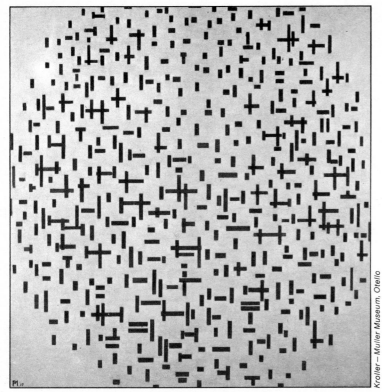

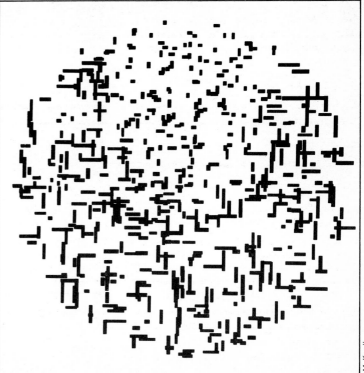

National Gallery

produced in 1964 by the psychologist A. M. Noll. In an interesting experiment in which a hundred people of different backgrounds and different attitudes to art were shown both pictures, only 28 percent correctly identified them. Perhaps even more surprising, of the people who liked abstract art, 76 percent preferred the computer picture!

Of course, the computer had to be "instructed" to create a certain kind of pattern, so the human element was present in the composition and we do not know what Mondrian might have produced had he had access to a computer, but the results are intriguing. Sir Herbert Read, in discussing the evaluation of art, admitted, "Frankly, I do not know how we are to judge form except by the same instinct that creates it." It is not surprising, then, that there is room for some disagreement.

There are many paintings of undisputed greatness. Consider Leonardo da Vinci's *Virgin of the Rocks*. Special knowledge of history, the development of painting, the man himself, can all add to appreciation of a picture; color too is a vital part of our experience of painting; and a reproduction is a shadow of the original. Form, however, is the overriding concern and translates well even in monochrome.

At first, the content of the picture dominates our senses; you will find yourself paying special attention to the faces of the subjects—and if you know that the young Leonardo was separated early from his beautiful mother, the Madonna's face has a particularly haunting quality. As you look, details spring into focus—there is so much to delight and to be discovered. When you have explored the picture, possibly coming back to it several times, hold it farther away and let your eyes travel over the forms.

The basic shape is triangular, rising not to a sharp peak but a rounded finish. See how the motif is repeated, with variations, throughout the canvas. The arrangement of figures is not perfectly triangular, but breaks into slight irregularity with the head of the angel. Balance and surprise are integrated into a complex and deeply satisfying unity. The more you look at this painting, the more you will understand why it has been acclaimed.

Turn back to the two paintings at the beginning. Can you now see differences between them that were not apparent before? Let your own responses come through—what you like *is* what art is all about.

all periods of history, and every person has the innate capacity to respond to them.

When we first look at a picture, we are concerned with the subject depicted, whether it is a nude woman, a vase of flowers or a can of soup, and we may not immediately be aware of the forms as something apart. Many modern paintings dispense with the attempt to portray objects and go straight through to "abstract" forms

—a highly sophisticated technique and one that many people find confusing.

Compare the two abstract pictures on the preceding page. Consider them in terms of balance and surprise. Which is "better"?

One was produced by a computer, one by the Dutch artist Piet Mondrian. Which is which? The picture on the left is Mondrian's *Composition with Lines* (1917); the other was computer-

The spellbinders

From the sacred mushroom to tobacco, drugs have always been used by witch doctors to transcend reality and to use their experience to benefit the tribe. It is now becoming accepted that some drugs, by liberating mind from body, give the user extrasensory perception. Certainly many medicine men genuinely believe that they possess second sight after taking drugs.

The witch doctor, bizarre as he may seem to Western eyes, is not merely a fluke of nature. He performs definite and necessary social functions, and if he is not endowed from birth with the special talent for communication with spirits, then he must be trained, like any "professional" person.

Occasionally there was the "natural," chosen because he could go voluntarily into what would now be described as a trance state. In this state, it was believed, he would have access to information from the spirit world.

But, when there was no natural talent of this kind (which was most often the case), witch doctors had to be trained. As soon as some young man showed signs of having the required ability, he would be put through a course of physical and spiritual exercises designed to enable him to go into a trance when required.

If even training of this kind could not produce the desired results, artificial aids were introduced. Music, dancing, drumming, rhythm of any kind, were used to help the witch doctor shake off his conscious self. So were plant drugs.

Drugs were also used in primitive societies, as they are in every civilization, for a variety of purposes—as medicines, as energizers and as tranquilizers. But their most important function was to enable men to lose their everyday selves. They believed they were leaving their bodies although, to the casual observer, it more often seemed as if they were taking leave of their senses, losing their wits.

The fly agaric fungus or *Amanita muscaria* (left) and *Ipomea cairica* (right), a member of the morning glory family. Such plants were used to cure illnesses of the soul, to divine the future and to gain supernatural knowledge. The sacred mushroom, used to train shamans or witch doctors, is said to conjure up paradise. The seeds of the morning glory, which contain a relative of lysergic acid (LSD), induce visions.

When Columbus and his men reached the New World, they found many such drugs in use. For a time they assumed the drugs had the same function as beer and wine in the Old World—intoxication. But gradually they were compelled to realize that the effects of the drugs were not the same as those produced by alcohol. The purpose of the drugs was to help the Indian medicine man to see visions and hear voices, which were presumed to come from the spirit world. The tribe relied upon these manifestations as an advisory service—which told them what to do to defeat their enemies or combat disease.

"Among other evil practices," Fernandez de Oviedo remarked in one of the earliest accounts of the American Indians to be published in Europe, "the Indians have one that is especially harmful, inhaling a certain kind of smoke, which they call tobacco, in order to produce a state of stupor." It is a little difficult today, when tobacco is used only as a mild stimulant or to assist relaxation, for us to

Jane Burton/Bruce Colman

Dorothy Myers/Bruce Colman

understand why it should have been regarded in America as a hallucinogenic drug. Yet in those days it was the one most widely used of all plant drugs to induce trances, as, indeed, it still is among primitive tribes in Central and South America.

The Indians relied on it, in particular, in the training of medicine men. Visiting Guiana a century ago, the explorer Everard Im Thurn found that, when old enough to be initiated into a tribe, youths were compelled to withdraw from the village for a time, to live alone and to fast, except for tobacco juice mixed with water. Watchers reported whether, "maddened by the draughts of nicotine and by the terrors of his long solitary wanderings," any particular youth could work himself up into sufficient frenzy to go into a trance and communicate with the spirits. If he could, he would be trained as a medicine man.

Cactus Kick

Although tobacco was the commonest drug in use for this purpose, it was not regarded as the best. More powerful drugs were used if they happened to grow locally. Of these, the peyotl cactus has since been made familiar through its derivative mescaline. This is the drug Aldous Huxley experimented with, and it formed the basis of his book *The Doors of Perception*.

Huxley saw everyday objects as if in a new light, their shapes and colors transformed rather than changed. But the Mexican medicine man used peyotl, when he could find it, for positive spiritual purposes which Carlos Castaneda has described in his best-selling *Teachings of Don Juan* and its successors. Their aim was to reach a different level of reality, transcending time and space.

The Spanish colonists did not doubt for a moment that peyotl had this power. Again and again, they reported instances. The great seventeenth century Spanish botanist Francisco Hernandez, for example, described how, after taking peyotl, the Indian could "foresee and predict anything"

South American shamans smoked large quantities of tobacco to achieve ecstatic experiences or just for pleasure. A Brazilian Indian (left) enjoys a cigar, his red eyes hinting that he is in a trance. Some tribes still take drugs for the visions they cause. A common sight is this Indian chief (right), his state of consciousness altered through drugs, sitting in a trance.

—whether an enemy tribe was planning to attack, who had stolen some missing household goods "and other things of this sort." The chronicler Father Joseph d'Acosta agreed; peyotl enabled a man to report battles "200 or 300 leagues (several hundred miles) distant, on the very day they took place, or the day after."

Reports of these powers disturbed both the Spanish authorities and the Spanish priests. The Inquisition was called in, with the result that making peyotl was formally denounced as "an act of superstition, to be condemned as opposed to the purity and integrity of the holy Catholic faith." In reciting their catechisms, Mexican converts (and it was unwise, with the Inquisition around, not to become one) were asked, among other questions:

"Dost thou foretell events by reading signs, or interpreting dreams, or by water, making circles and figures on the surface? Dost thou suck the blood of others, or dost thou wander about at night, calling upon the demon to help thee? Hast thou drunk peyotl, or hast thou given it to others to drink, in order to find out secrets or to discover where lost or stolen articles were?"

As it was not advisable to answer "yes" to any of these questions, the cult of peyotl was forced under-

Camera Press

ground, out of the open.

In many parts of America, however, and particularly in and around Mexico, there were too many plant drugs available for prohibition to be effective. The powerful seeds of the morning glory were particularly valued for their ability to induce visions. So were certain types of mushroom and datura, better known as jimson weed.

Mushroom Madness

The Swiss naturalist J. J. von Tschudi, who went to Peru in the 1840s, watched a tribal medicine man who had taken datura go into what appeared to be an epileptic fit, after which he sank into a coma. But, "in the evening, when I saw him again, he was relating to a circle of attentive listeners the particulars of his vision, during which he alleged he had held communication with the spirits of his forefathers."

Von Tschudi was probably as responsible as anybody for creating a new respect for what plant drugs could do. Previously the stories about them had been dismissed as "travelers' tales," a term which still carries a derisory note today. One of the best known had come out of Siberia in the eighteenth century when a Swedish colonel, Count von Strahlenberg, came back from a long spell as prisoner of war in Siberia to report that some tribesmen there greatly relished the red-capped *Amanita muscaria*, or fly agaric mushroom, in order to induce visions.

But, in that rationalist era, the only part of his story to attract attention was his description of the way the poorer members of the tribe held out begging bowls to receive, not the alms, but the urine of those rich enough to afford the mushrooms. For, when the urine was drunk, it, too, produced visions, up to the third or fourth time around. Even the reindeer, it was reported, could become addicted to agaric urine, which herdsmen found a useful inducement at rounding up time.

The story received wide publicity in Europe at the time, but was not believed because everyone assumed fly agaric to be poisonous. It was not until more than a century later that reports from academically respectable investigators confirmed the truth of the story.

Anthropologists found plant drugs had become so important in some communities that they were actually worshiped in their own right. In Peru, a "Coca Momma," corresponding to the "Earth Mother" in other parts of the world, was held as a minor deity. The Vedic poems show that Soma was worshiped as a god in India. They do not, however, clearly reveal what soma was. Some commentators suggest hashish, others opium. In his book on the subject, the American banker R. G. Wasson puts forward the claims of the fly agaric mushroom, which certainly fits the Vedic descriptions better than do the other two.

He has also shown that another species of mushroom is regarded as a god, or a spirit, by some Mexican tribes. They had concealed the existence of their mushroom cult so effectively from the Spanish colonial government—and from the Inquisition —that everyone assumed it was extinct. Field workers eventually uncovered it in the 1930s and Wasson, on investigation, found the mushroom had acquired a status roughly equivalent to that of the spiritualist medium's "guide" or "control."

Second Sight

The medicine man, Wasson realized, plays a relatively minor part in the cult. His function had diminished to that of allowing the mushroom spirit to speak through him when the tribe needed advice on such issues as how to treat a sick man or how to find a missing donkey.

Both in Mexico and in Siberia, the mushroom's voice has been personified so that there are assumed to be mushroom men and mushroom women in the spirit world. Interestingly, they are pictured as being the same size as the mushrooms which are eaten.

This ties in with European folklore, in which mushrooms, or toadstools, have become a prominent stage property, with elves and fairies frequently using them to sit on. It also suggests that mushroom cults must have existed in Europe at some time in history or prehistory.

Perhaps the authorities suppressed them because they represented a threat to their peace of mind. After all, a chief who was planning a purge of potential rivals cannot have liked the possibility they might divine his intentions simply by eating a few mushrooms.

But, at the time anthropology was coming into its own a century ago, divination, or foretelling the future, was assumed to be a myth. As a result, hardly anyone took seriously the drugs used to promote it. The exceptions were a handful of individuals impressed by the evidence, just as the

Spanish priests had been convinced that, under the influence of peyotl or mushrooms, some men really could foretell the future.

One of these exceptions was Dr. Rafael Bayon, who worked in Peru in the early years of this century. He found that local missionaries had no doubt that a certain plant drug, yage, could give a man second sight. One of Bayon's colleagues, the commandant in charge of a local army detachment, offered himself as a guinea pig for an experiment. Bayon described what happened in *The Times* in 1912:

"He took the tincture at night in a jar of water, and, in the morning, at reveille, he came to me with the news of the death of his father, who lived in Ibague, and of the illness of his little sister, whom he loved very dearly. All this, he declared, he had seen during the night. No one had arrived who could have communicated such news to him, and the nearest post or telegraph office is at least fifteen days' journey away. About a month after this strange vision, a courier happened to arrive with letters which announced to him the death of his father and the recovery of his sister from a serious illness."

Such stories were common, but orthodox anthropology shied away from them for many years as "anecdotal" and unscientific. Recently, however, there have been signs of a growing disposition to accept that some of them, at least, may have been true; that certain drugs, by liberating the mind from the body, are capable of providing extrasensory perception. Certainly, medicine men who still use them genuinely believe that they give second sight, and the American anthropologist Douglas Sharon has given another account of how one of them works in *Flesh of the Gods.*

Trance Enhanced

"Galvaez, the Peruvian folk healer, uses tobacco when he wants simply to speed up his imaginative processes, to clear his mind, but he takes the San Pedro cactus when he wants to put himself out of his mind, into a trance. This brings a detachment, a type of visual force in the individual inclusive of all the senses—seeing, hearing, smelling, touching, all the senses, including the sixth sense, the telepathic sense of transmitting oneself across time and matter." Through this sixth sense Galvaez can distinguish and resolve problems at a distance or "see" physical symptoms within the body, as if by an X-ray, and

prescribe how best to deal with them.

Assuming, for argument's sake, that some drugs can liberate the sixth sense, the question remains, How? The answer seems to be that the drug is only the catalyst, or trigger. What happens in our minds is conditioned by the degree of our own receptivity, rather than by the pharmacological action of the drug.

A Bad Trip

When theological students at Harvard were tested recently with one of the hallucinogenic mushrooms, for example, they came up with accounts of mystical experiences which largely duplicated accounts of mystical experiences of Christian saints they had read in books. Takers of mescaline commonly have similar experiences to Huxley's, just as Huxley's were similar to those reported by earlier experimenters like Havelock Ellis.

But on some people the effects are very different, particularly when the drug is taken in the original Mexican context. On other people, such drugs have no perceptible effect, except to make them sick. That is what happened to William James, who wrote to his brother Henry, the novelist, saying was prepared in future to take the mescaline visions on trust. A few people also have unpleasant reactions —"bad trips"—with depressing and sometimes terrifying hallucinations.

This is not surprising—or should not be. We are familiar, after all, with the exceedingly diverse ways friends and acquaintances can be affected by alcohol. It is not the drug, but the human reaction to it, which matters.

And this helps to explain why the role of the same drug can vary so greatly in different communities. The effects depend very largely on the expectations people have of them. When tobacco was introduced into Europe in the sixteenth century, it was primarily as a medicine, and it enjoyed an enormous vogue, being recommended for every disorder from pneumonia to the pox. Later, Walter Raleigh helped to popularize it as a fashionable pastime. In doing so he aroused the ire of James I, who wrote his *Counterblaste to Tobacco* to try to check the craze.

But although the king listed a score of reasons why tobacco smoking was pernicious, its tendency to induce trances and visions was not one of them. Nobody in Europe expected to get visions from it. Nobody, so far as is known, ever did. Yet in America the medicine men continued to use it for that purpose, and do so to this day.

All you want to know about...
SEXUAL BEHAVIOR

Camera Press

Q WHAT IS IMPOTENCE?

A Impotence in men basically takes three forms: the inability to develop an erection in the presence of a woman, inability to sustain it to allow vaginal intercourse to take place, and premature ejaculation, which allows only a few seconds of intercourse to take place. All men have at some time in their sex lives suffered from one or other of these forms of impotence, and with very rare exceptions, where physical illness is involved, the causes are largely psychological. As with the female orgasm, impotence is generally a matter of commitment to the sex act. This lack of commitment may be due to any one of a vast number of reasons, many of which can be sorted out as the result of a discussion with a psychologist or doctor. An even larger number will disappear as the result of a frank discussion with one's wife or girlfriend. The most common reason for lack of commitment is a belief that the sex act itself is somehow "wrong." Guilt associated with sex (sex is "dirty" or "nasty and

shouldn't be done with nice girls") is a good example of this. More frequently the lack of commitment may be because of a feeling that somehow the novelty has worn off—the wife or girlfriend, who once seemed so tantalizing, has now become predictable, dull and available. It may also be caused by an unconscious aggression —a need to humiliate or punish the partner. One of the most common reasons, however, for this lack of commitment is that the impotent person is, in some other bedroom, already committing himself fully to someone else!

HOW MANY PEOPLE SUFFER FROM IMPOTENCE OR FRIGIDITY?

In all probability all adults have suffered from occasional brushes with sexual inadequacy of this kind. If one includes premature ejaculation, which is one of the most common forms of impotence, then some estimates imply that 50 percent of men suffer enough from impotence for it to be a nuisance to them. Of this figure, only 5 percent are suffering from physiological causes of impotence—the kind that may be dependent upon old age or

some unavoidable physical change. For women the problem is somewhat more difficult to settle because of the enormous variation in their ability to achieve orgasm. Some women are fortunate enough to manage it on almost every occasion, but probably the majority are not so lucky. Minor orgasms which follow a successful and happy period of love-making are often the best that can be achieved, and some women declare that they feel physically and psychologically satisfied by such experiences. Men and women with total impotence or complete frigidity are the really unfortunate ones and, physical disabilities apart, they constitute a small proportion of the population—certainly less than one in twenty.

HOW CAN PEOPLE GET OVER IMPOTENCE?

Simply by restoring the sense of commitment. If one is suffering from the "sex is nasty" hang-up—almost always instilled during childhood by inhibited parents—then a fairly ruthless reeducational program is required, and this will need to be handled by a specially trained psychotherapist. If lack of novelty is the problem, then both partners should use a bit of imagination. Erotic literature—long out of general fashion in the Western world and yet a vital part of Asian love and marriage culture—can work wonders. Unconscious aggressions, on the other hand, are less easily dealt with because by their nature they are difficult to pin down and identify. Frank talking between husband and wife is at least the first step. Finally, when the problem is that the impotent person has acquired a lover who is already receiving the full quota of commitment, then matters are fairly serious. Perhaps the best bet here is for the dull wife to change back into the exciting mistress that she once was (or should have been).

WHAT IS FRIGIDITY?

Frigidity is an unfortunately chosen word which seems to suggest coldness on the part of the woman, and a hatred or dislike of sex. In fact it really refers to a woman's inability to gain genuine satisfaction from the sex act (on the whole that means not having an orgasm). In many ways it parallels male impotence, with the exception that most frigid women will be able to participate in sex even if they fail to have an orgasm. Some may even simulate an orgasm, in order to please their lover. No impotent man can "simulate" an erect penis of course, and the effects of prolonged impotence therefore tend to be psychologically more disturbing to the male's self-esteem than prolonged frigidity is to the woman's. A special type of frigidity in women called vaginismus, which consists of a strong contraction of the vaginal muscles, can prevent the penis from entering and thus prevent intercourse from taking place. The principal cause of frigidity, as with male impotence, is psychological, and while there may be a number of causes—ignorance, taboos instilled in early childhood, fear of getting pregnant, unconscious dislike of one's lover, etc.—these can all be summed up as involving a lack of commitment to the sex act itself. The state of sexual arousal which leads through intercourse to orgasm and ultimate satisfaction consists of a combination of hundreds, perhaps thousands, of physiological and psychological processes, but in essence they involve commitment at three centers—the mind, the heart and the genital organs. For a completely satisfactory sex act, the partner must be wanted in these three dimensions of love, and when one of the dimensions is missing the sex act will be at best a partial success. Unfortunately there are no hard and fast rules for achieving commitment on these three levels—for human beings are highly complex organisms and not simple machines. Frank and open-hearted discussions between lovers can often overcome some of the problems causing frigidity by relieving the tensions which themselves are standing in the way of commitment. Psychological advice can also be sought if the problems seem particularly deep-seated, and, as with male impotence, psychotherapy has a very high success record. Often the act of committing oneself to seek assistance, which itself implies a realization of the need for a new attitude to sex, puts one well on the road to achieving that *total* commitment which is the heart of the matter.

HOW BIG IS THE NORMAL PENIS?

The size of the penis in males is much more constant than most people seem to believe. The measurements that really matter concern the erect penis, the average size of which is between 5½ and 6½ inches, with extremes ranging between 4½ and 8 inches. The average circumference is approximately 4 inches. Contrary to much folklore, women's sexual satisfaction is *not* dependent upon penis size, as the clitoris, the focal point of feminine sexual pleasure, will be stimulated adequately by any erect male organ. If this fact were better known, the number of men seeking psychological advice because of impotence caused by feelings of "embarrassment" about penis size would be dramatically reduced.

SHOULD MENSTRUATION AFFECT YOUR SEX LIFE?

There are probably more myths and old wives' tales about menstruation than almost any other facet of sexual behavior. These include the absurd beliefs that you should not bathe, swim, wash your hair or take vigorous exercise during the menstrual period, but most women today seem to reject these prohibitions. Mysteriously there is still a common feeling that sexual behavior itself should cease during menstruation. In point of fact, apart from the slight messiness caused by bleeding, both partners can enjoy a completely satisfactory love relationship during menstruation and normal intercourse need not be interfered with at all. In the case of women on the pill, whose menstrual bleeding is very significantly reduced anyway, the prohibitions are even less meaningful. One very important and enormously widespread belief is that it is impossible to become pregnant as the result of intercourse during menstruation. This is totally incorrect, and many couples have been given an unpleasant surprise in the form of an unwanted pregnancy through holding to it. The probability of conception taking place as the result of intercourse during menstruation is in fact significantly less than at other times of the month, but it is *not* reduced to zero.

WHAT IS THE CLITORIS?

The clitoris is the female equivalent of the penis. During the foreplay leading up to intercourse and while lovemaking is taking place it becomes engorged with blood, erect and enormously sensitive. Although it is very much smaller than the penis, it contains approximately the same number of sensory nerve endings and is thus a highly charged and erotically sensitive organ. It and the tissues surrounding it also provide a lubricating fluid which allows smooth movements of the penis in the vagina to take place. Orgasm, when it occurs, is followed by a slow collapse of the clitoris, again comparable to the loss of erection in the penis which follows male orgasm.

HOW DOES THE MENOPAUSE AFFECT YOUR SEX LIFE?

The menopause occurs once a woman ceases ovulation, and from that moment on she will be unable to have any children. This itself need not prevent her from leading a full sex life, but because of the great physiological changes taking place in her body and her psychological realization that one important part of her life is ended, there is often a temporary period of depression in which her sexual responsiveness is diminished. Such a short-term depression is quite normal, and afterwards many women find themselves unexpectedly liberated and able to enjoy a new freedom in sexual relationships because the fear of pregnancy is totally banished. The usual time for the menopause is the late forties, and if a couple can free themselves from the old-fashioned notion that sexual vigor will decline rapidly from this moment, most couples should be able to look forward to two decades of a happy sex life ahead of them. There is in fact a male equivalent to the menopause which is related to the moment when a man's reproductive organs cease to produce fertile sperm. Reproductive ability in the male does decline slowly with age, but it may not cease before the seventies or even the eighties. Even this may not mean the end of love and its physical fulfillment through sex.

WHAT ARE THE ADVANTAGES OF CIRCUMCISION?

This practice, which involves the surgical removal of the foreskin of the penis, has origins which lie back in the mists of antiquity. It is widely practiced in many primitive societies at the time of the onset of puberty when the ability of the young man to withstand the pain and obvious psychological trauma of a ritual circumcision is counted as denoting his transition from childhood to manhood. Grotesque practices of this kind rarely emerge in society without some reason however, and there are in fact two possible practical advantages to circumcision. The first, which is debatable at best, is that the removal of the foreskin, by ultimately reducing the sensitivity of the penis, allows the circumcised male to prolong sexual intercourse significantly. This argument may have some validity, but it should be remembered that the principal causes of premature ejaculation are psychological and not physical, and that most males, with or without foreskins, can generally learn to inhibit ejaculation until the required time. The second concerns the fact that in the course of time the foreskin builds up a deposit of a soapy substance, called smegma, which can solidify and become painful, if the interior of the foreskin is not regularly washed. Simple hygiene will seem to many to be a more satisfactory alternative to circumcision, but it is perhaps significant that cancer of the penis —not a particularly common condition fortunately—hardly ever occurs in circumcised males.

WHAT GOVERNS THE FREQUENCY OF SEXUAL INTERCOURSE?

Basically the answer is—desire and demand. Again, contrary to much folklore, human variation in the need for sexual intercourse is not all that great. The physiological capacity to make love with orgasm does fall off slightly in men from a peak period in adolescence until some time in the fifties or sixties, and then a more rapid decline. This sexual potential however is seldom completely exploited—in other words people rarely, if ever, make love to the full extent of their physiological capabilities. In practical terms therefore, decline in physiological capacity with age need not—provided that one maintains a psychologically healthy interest in sex—lead to a reduction in the amount of love-making. It is for this reason that as long as the appropriate stimuli are present (a desirable and responsive partner), there does not have to be a vast difference between the frequency of sexual intercourse in different human beings. Attitudes to sex make a huge difference however. Western society is slowly easing out of a period in which it was generally believed that the prime function and hence the only justification for sex was the propagation of children, and sex for sex's sake was considered to be improper or even "sinful." Psychologists now recognize the considerable psychological benefits which go hand in hand with a contented sex life, and there is also a growing acceptance of sex as an important form of "play" or "recreation." Such attitudes will obviously have an effect on the frequency with which people make love. Recent surveys and polls of sexual habits, incidentally, suggest that the average married couple who have been living together for more than a year or so settle down to a pattern of love-making which "averages out" at about twice a week.

WHAT IS MEANT BY INFANTILE SEXUALITY?

This phrase was coined by the great psychoanalyst Sigmund Freud, and it caused a great sensation when he first referred to it. To people living in Victorian times, when it was fashionable to consider sexual behavior to be tainted with sin, the idea of associating sex with the innocence of childhood was considered outrageous. Freud of course was not trying to imply that infants or even young children had a psychological awareness of sexual behavior in the adult sense, but was merely pointing out that children were born with an instinctive drive of great power, initially undirected but which would later be channeled, by learning and experience, into the patterns of sexual behavior which were appropriate to the society. In its early stages the drive is largely concerned with the formation of a magnetic bond between mother and child. Later, with the arrival of physiological maturity and capacity to reproduce children, the drive would push the individual into forming a mating relationship with a member of the opposite sex. Of course there is no doubt that from a very early age children find that stroking or touching their sexual organs is a pleasurable experience and this rudimentary form of masturbation is a perfectly natural aspect of a child's development. The point to realize is that the period from infancy to adulthood is a kind of sexual instruction course in which the instinctive pleasure that is experienced when the sexual organs are manipulated is transformed into a powerful and wonderfully exciting method of propagating the species.

WHAT IS THE MOST EFFECTIVE METHOD OF BIRTH CONTROL?

The most effective method is sterilization, which is achieved as the result of a minor but more or less irreversible surgical operation for men and women. The least effective, and easily the worst psychologically, is the so-called withdrawal technique, in which the penis is removed from the vagina before ejaculation. The disastrous failure rate of this method depends principally upon two factors: the difficulty of insuring that withdrawal occurs in time, and because fertile sperm often exist in the "lubricating fluid" which emerges from the penis during intercourse and well before ejaculation. Psychologically, *coitus interruptus*, as it is called, is particularly unsatisfactory for the woman, who can seldom achieve orgasm. There are numerous other methods of birth control of varying degrees of efficiency. For most modern women the pill is probably the most satisfactory; though, contrary to common belief, it is not an absolutely safe method. "Natural" methods, such as those which rely on the use of the "safe period" and depend upon a very precise knowledge by the woman of when she is ovulating, have a high failure rate and are not recommended unless there are strong religious convictions about physical forms of birth control. Other methods, such as the cap, condoms, spermicidal creams, intrauterine devices like the coil, may be particularly suited to individuals or specific occasions, but the best method for any individual will be arrived at as the result of medical consultation and the consideration of personal circumstances.

Mansell Collection

Darwin: tidal wave

At school, Charles Darwin's intellect was regarded as somewhat below average. Yet his theories on the evolution of man, published following a five-year voyage as unpaid naturalist on the ship *Beagle*, established him as a great scientific thinker.

In the middle of the nineteenth century, in secure, staid Victorian England, one of the great leaps forward in man's understanding of the universe and his place within it took place. For, on November 24, 1859, came the publication of Darwin's *The Origin of Species*, called by William Irvine, in his *Apes, Angels and Victorians*, the most important book of the century.

The accepted attitude of that time was that species were unchangeable. Animals and plants were just as they were when they were created in the Garden of Eden for the especial benefit of man, whom God had placed in dominion over them all. To prove that they were changeable, that they had been changed and were indeed still in the process of change, was to throw doubt on the word of God and undermine religious faith. Milton's verse:

The Earth obey'd and straight
Op'ning her fertile womb,
    teem'd at birth
Innumerous living creatures,
    perfect forms,
Limb'd and full grown . . .

expressed the view that had generally been accepted since the Middle Ages and which was now to be overthrown.

At first sight Charles Darwin seems an unlikely person to have come up with such startling theories. He was the son of a prosperous physician with a practice at Shrewsbury, Shropshire. And he was, according to his autobiography, "considered by the masters and by my father as a very ordinary boy, rather below the common standard of intellect."

At Edinburgh, where he was sent to study medicine, he found himself bored by the lectures, nauseated by dissection and appalled when he watched two operations, performed before the days of chloroform. From Edinburgh he was sent to Christ's College, Cambridge, with the vague idea of going into the Church. Charles ambled through his degree course, collected beetles, shells, insects and other natural history objects with enthusiasm, engaged with even greater enthusiasm in shooting parties, and took up geology. He also formed a close friendship with a professor of botany, the Reverend

John Steven Henslow, which was to have far-reaching consequences on the course of his life and on science.

So far there were few signs of genius in Darwin, though his genes might today be considered auspicious. His grandfather was Erasmus Darwin, author of the philosophical poem *Zoonomia*, which set out to unravel not only the theory of disease but the secrets of life itself, and which in some ways foreshadowed evolution. And his mother was Susannah Wedgwood, daughter of the great innovative potter Josiah Wedgwood. Charles Darwin's wife was also a Wedgwood: Emma, his cousin, daughter of his uncle Josiah Wedgwood II.

Voyage into the Unknown

In the August of 1831, eight months after he had obtained his degree, Charles Darwin, then 22, was recommended by Henslow for the post of unpaid naturalist to the ship *Beagle*. His father at first demurred, but was persuaded to let Charles take up the offer by his uncle Josiah. The *Beagle*, a 242-ton, 90-foot brig, was to make a five-year voyage charting the coast of South America and carrying out a chain of chronological reckonings around the world in order to get a more accurate fixing of longitude.

History is made by a coming together of vital circumstances, the right man arriving at the right place at the right time. Certainly scientific history was made because this young man, with talents as yet unproven though confidently believed in by Henslow, set out on a remarkable voyage which provided him with unique opportunities to exercise his talents. These included abilities as a collector of natural history data, as observer and recorder, and, both during the voyage and afterwards, as profound thinker, at a time when the world was just about ready, in the face of convincing evidence, to accept the overturning of long-held beliefs.

Darwin certainly did not invent or discover evolution. The idea that life descends from simpler forms is as old as Aristotle, and professional scientists as well as amateurs in the eighteenth century had speculated widely on geology, on fossils, and on

Charles Darwin's theories on evolution altered beliefs about the origin of species. He argued that all living things had evolved from simpler forms of life present millions of years ago and that man sprang from the stock of apes.

Mansell Collection

creation. There were the Neptunists, who believed that all rocks except volcanic ones were formed of matter deposited from water; and the Plutonists, who insisted that rocks were the result of earthquakes.

Catastrophism, the doctrine which proposed the successive destruction of the face of the earth by violent and supernatural upheavals, was superseded by a proposition made by James Hutton (1726-97). He put forward the idea that phenomena of geology are the products of forces that are still in operation around us: hills and mountains are not everlasting but have been sculptured by slow processes of erosion that are still at work; and alluvial sediment is being continuously deposited on the sea bed. Observing that sedimentary rocks bear all the evidence of having been similarly deposited, he deduced from their thickness that the time scale involved was immense.

Survival of the Fittest

His work came to be extended and developed by Sir Charles Lyell, a friend of Darwin's and later a supporter of the theory of evolution; he christened this theory Uniformitarianism. The main principle was that the past history of the earth must be explained by what can be seen to be happening now.

This then was Darwin's jumping-off point: a climate of gently speculative scientific thought with the local weather of entrenched religious beliefs, firmly based on a literal interpretation of the Bible. *The Origin of Species* was to have the effect of a tidal wave.

Throughout the years of the *Beagle*'s voyage, all the things Darwin observed and investigated and recorded drew him inevitably to the conclusion that all forms of vegetable and animal life, past and present, have been produced by a series of gradual changes in natural descent from parents to offspring. He also concluded that all the animals have descended from four or five progenitors, all plants from a similar number. This theory was combined with a development of the Malthusian theory, which proposed that deaths from famine or disasters reduced the numbers of each kind of living thing and so prevented overpopulation.

Darwin developed this idea to evolve his own theory of natural selection or "the survival of the fittest"—that is that the offspring of weaker individuals, those least fitted for their environment, would not survive to perpetuate their kind. Thus the race would be preserved by individuals of exceptional vigor and superior qualities. These superior parents, by interbreeding and through sexual selection, continually develop and intensify their better features, and eventually become markedly different, ultimately forming a new species.

Evidence accrued all the time as the *Beagle* made her way around the world, but most startlingly so at the Galapagos Islands, which were reached in 1835. These ten remote black lava islands, by the circumstance of their situation, formed a perfect natural laboratory of evolution. The depth of the sea between them and their volcanic origin indicated that they had never been united. The strong currents that ran between them were in such a direction that it was unlikely that seeds or eggs would be borne from island to island, and there were no strong winds to transfer life either. Few migrant plants or animals would have been able to reach the Galapagos. And once they had done so they would not have been able to move to other islands in the group.

So despite the fact that the islands were separated by no more than 50 or 60 miles, and although all the species bore a close resemblance to those of South America, 500 miles away, they were nevertheless markedly different. Not only were many of them unique to the Galapagos Islands—they were unique from island to island.

Evolution

"It was most striking," wrote Darwin, "to be surrounded by new birds, new reptiles, new shells, new insects, new plants, and yet—by innumerable trifling details of structure and even by the tones of voice and plumage of the birds—to have the temperate plains of Patagonia or the hot deserts of Chile brought vividly before my eyes." He concluded that the archipelago, though standing in the Pacific Ocean, was zoologically part of America and had evolved its own forms of flora and fauna through environmental adjustments.

Darwin also noted that because the islands were isolated and no competitors had arrived to upset the ecological balance, some animals, for example the woodpecker finch, had been able to adapt in directions that would otherwise have been closed to them. Isolation had encouraged the production of new species.

In Patagonia, at Punta Alba, Darwin had found fossils of megatheroid animals which had become extinct millennia ago—such as the giant armadillo, Mylodon—and he noticed that all bore close resemblance to their smaller, modern counterparts. At a fossil bed near Port Julia he found the fossil bones of an animal as large as a camel with an elongated neck, like a llama, but with the build of a rhinoceros. He realized that these were the bones of the ancestor of the modern llamas which were all around him—a link between the living and the extinct species. By the time Darwin got home again, in 1836, he had become aware that the similarities and differences of earth's creatures were the result of their having descended from common ancestors.

Stunning Revelations

Once back from his five-year voyage, although Darwin produced a journal of his voyage which was ready two years after his return and which sold well, he worked only slowly on what was to become *The Origin of Species*. In fact he continued to collect evidence from all quarters—though he himself never again stirred from the confines of his secluded house at Downe in Kent.

One really wonders if he would ever have considered he had finished work on what William Irvine called "his patient and laborious heresy" had he not in 1857 been given a severe jolt. A naturalist called Alfred Russell Wallace who was working in the Malay archipelago corresponded with Darwin about his own theories on evolution. Darwin replied courteously and cautiously, mentioning that he had been working on the subject for 20 years. But in 1858 Wallace sent him an essay, to be sent on to Lyell, called *On the Tendencies of Varieties to Depart Infinitely from the Original Type*, which contained exactly the same theory as Darwin's.

Darwin had produced, at Lyell's urgent request, an abstract of his theory some years earlier, and several of Darwin's close friends knew of his work. So, although Darwin himself was prepared to stand aside lest he be thought "to have behaved in a paltry spirit," in the end both Wallace's paper and Darwin's 1844 abstract, plus a letter he had written in 1857 to Asa Gray, the American botanist, were jointly presented to the Linnaean Society.

The learned society was silent and stunned at what it heard. One member, George Bentham, withdrew a paper he had intended to read on the fixity of species.

Within the image:

MOSES OR DARWIN.

"MONKEYVILLE" TRIAL SCENES.

BOOK OF GENESIS.

JUDGE READS STORY OF CREATION TO JURY.

Modernism was put on its trial yesterday at Dayton, a small town of 20,000 inhabitants, in Tennessee, U.S.A. The prosecutor is **Orthodoxy**.

It is no mock trial, but serious business with an army of famous lawyers on each side and a young man, John T. Scopes, in the dock.

Scopes taught his class at the local high school that the Darwinian theory of evolution is right. This is against the law of Tennessee, and Scopes was indicted.

If Scopes is convicted, the case will be carried to the Supreme Court. The first (Dayton) act in the farce may last several weeks.

Little was done at the opening of the ...

The Ascent of Man

Dayton, Tennessee, and the long hot summer of 1925. In the courthouse, America's historic "Monkey Trial" is being fought over Darwin's theory of evolution. Is man really descended from the apes? In the witness stand schoolteacher Scopes (left), prosecuted by ultraconservative William Jennings Bryan (right), waits anxiously for the verdict, a verdict for him and for all mankind.

John Thomas Scopes was an ordinary enough local schoolteacher, not at all the kind of man you would expect to make history. But, in the hot summer of 1925, his name swept around the world. At Dayton, Tennessee, 24-year-old Scopes was charged with "undermining the peace and dignity of the state" by teaching his pupils Darwin's theory of evolution, that man had descended from the apes.

The case, which newspapers throughout the world quickly dubbed "The Monkey Trial," arose because the people of Dayton were largely devout members of one of America's most fanatical religious sects, the Fundamentalists. They believed in the literal interpretation of the Scriptures as history, and they had bulldozed a law through the State Senate, forbidding the teaching of the scientific evolution of man in any state school.

By quoting Darwin—and flying in the face of Genesis—John Thomas Scopes had broken that law.

The trial brought into opposition two of the most powerful men in the United States.

Leading the pro-Bible forces as special prosecutor was William Jennings Bryan, 65, thrice the Democratic presidential candidate. He saw the trial as a God-sent opportunity to strike down the "forces of darkness and spark off a Fundamentalist revival which could sweep him to the White House."

Facing him as defense counsel was

Robinson

U.P.I.

the man many Fundamentalists regarded as anti-Christ personified, Clarence Darrow, the nation's greatest criminal lawyer, who had devoted his life to defending hopeless causes—and winning.

The nub of Darrow's case was: "The Bible is a book primarily of religion and morals. It is not a book of science, never was and was never meant to be." Yet the Fundamentalist law passed in Tennessee "makes the Bible the yardstick to measure every man's intellect, to measure every man's intelligence and to measure every man's learning." This, thought Darrow, was misuse of the wisdom of the Bible.

Master Stroke

He did not propose to put Scopes himself on the stand. "What's the point?" asked Darrow. "Everything the prosecution has said about him is true." He did, however, propose to call expert witnesses to testify that the whole evolution of mankind could not be contained within the pages of Genesis.

The judge blocked that course on the grounds that the experts' evidence would be above the heads of the twelve good men and true—six Baptists, four Methodists, one Disciple of Christ and one other churchgoer—who made up the jury.

But Darrow pulled a master stroke

Although Clarence Darrow (right) lost his case in America's sensational "Monkey Trial," the indignation aroused by the verdict (later reversed) brought an end to anti-Darwinism in America.

when, after the court had adjourned to the open air because of the heat, he called Bryan, the special prosecutor himself, as a defense witness. Bryan, in the twin grip of his vanity and bigotry, accepted the challenge. Darrow made him look a fool in a series of exchanges of which one—the story of Joshua commanding the sun to stand still to lengthen the day—was typical:

Bryan: I believe what the Bible says. I accept it absolutely.
Darrow: So you believe the sun goes around the earth?
Bryan: No, I believe the earth goes around the sun.
Darrow: Now, Mr. Bryan, have you ever wondered what would have happened to the earth if it had stood still?
Bryan: No, the God I believe in could have taken care of that, Mr. Darrow.
Darrow: Don't you know it would have been converted into a molten mass of matter?
Bryan: I don't think I've ever had the question asked.
Darrow: Or ever thought about it!

But even Darrow's brilliant defense was not enough to overcome local

prejudice. Scopes was found guilty and fined $100 although the decision was later reversed on a technicality by the Tennessee Supreme Court. The trial, however, made Dayton a byword for parochial prejudice. Its citizens were described as "hayseeds" and "yokels." Fundamentalism and Bryan himself were destroyed by the most powerful of all weapons, ridicule—and, a month later, still in Dayton, Bryan collapsed and died from a stroke. The day, perhaps appropriately, was Sunday.

Monkey Business

". . . Is it true that we all come from monkeys?
When I look at you it must be so;
But if you're a monkey, where's your tail gone?
Eh, Dad? Don't you know?"

That Victorian popular song represents the lighter side of a controversy which began quietly but became bitter enough. It also represents the fallacious idea of what Darwin's theories actually said which did much to add to the bitterness: for Darwin did not say that man was descended from the apes. He postulated that modern man, and modern apes, had both descended from a common ancestral line, pursuing each their own evolutionary development.

It took six months, from publication of *The Origin of Species* in 1859, for the ferment to work itself into a froth. The froth boiled over at the famous meeting of the British Association at Oxford University in June 1860, when leading exponents were brought together to debate the theory of the origin of species. The clerical, anti-Darwin group was led by Samuel Wilberforce, nicknamed for his glib eloquence "Soapy Sam," who was bishop of Oxford. Darwin, absent through illness, was championed by T. H. Huxley with Hooker, director of Kew Gardens, as his second.

Wilberforce had been briefed by the anatomist Sir Richard Owen, a venomous enemy of Darwinism, and adopted his usual style of oratory, which leaned heavily on disparagement and sarcasm. He ridiculed Darwin's "casual theory," displaying great powers of mockery but little intellectual grasp of the theories he was deriding, and ended up by asking Huxley, rhetorically, whether it was "through his grandfather or his grandmother that he claimed descent from a monkey."

Decent Descent?

Huxley, audibly thanking the Lord for delivering his opponent into his hands, replied with dignity and authority, pointing out the Bishop's ignorance of the sciences involved, and ended up by remarking that though he would not be ashamed to have a monkey for his ancestor, he would be "ashamed to be connected with a man who used great gifts to obscure the truth."

The undergraduates, who had received the Bishop favorably enough, now swung around and applauded Huxley vociferously, while the clergy clamored for an apology, and one lady, with a finely developed sense of occasion, collapsed from shock. Battle was joined and raged fiercely for some years. But Darwin's carefully collected evidence was so strong that by the time *The Descent of Man and Selection in Relation to Sex* was published in 1871 most of the noisiest engagements were over.

Although *The Origin of Species* implied by inexorable logic that man is not the unique end to creation, God's masterpiece, in fact in that work Darwin avoided detailed reference to this, realizing that this aspect of his

Charles Darwin — a portrait. Darwin considered his success due to "the love of science, unbounded patience in long reflecting over any subject, industry in observing facts and a fair share of common sense."

theories was hedged about with prejudice. He did however hint at the inference to be drawn in one significant sentence: "Although in *The Origin of Species* the derivation of any particular species is never discussed, yet I thought it best, in order that no honorable man should accuse me of concealing my views, to add that by the work light should be thrown on the origin of man and his history."

A Similar Vein

In his *Principles of Geology*, a book which had accompanied Darwin around the world on board the *Beagle* and undoubtedly influenced him, Sir Charles Lyell had proclaimed evolution in the realms of botany and geology, but, with certain tact, designated a Creator of men and animals. Darwin was not the man to avoid the embarrassing consequences of his own thinking, and *The Descent of Man* is stimulating but controversial— "a special treatise on the origins of man," plus an important section on sexual selection, for which he had amassed a great deal of material.

Darwin pointed out the close similarity between the physical structure of a man and that of other animals: he drew comparison between the wing of a bird, the foreleg of a frog, the flipper of a whale and the arm of a man, and found in them, despite dissimilarities of function, great likeness

Mansell Collection

Keystone

in the patterns of the bones. There were more similarities in the muscles, the nerves, the blood vessels and the viscera—even in the convolutions of the brain.

Vestigial Remains

Then there was the extraordinary recapitulation of the evolution of the particular species shown in the embryonic development of an animal. "The embryos of a man, dog, seal, bat, reptile can at first hardly be distinguished from each other," Darwin wrote. He illustrated this most vividly by taking the embryos of a dog and a human at a similar stage of development, pointing out first their remarkable similarities, and second those transient reminders of former evolutionary stages in each. The gill arches recalled that the ancestors of both had once lived in the sea. In both embryos the heart was merely a simple, undivided pulsating vessel; and in each there was a tail—in man this would ultimately be no more than the *os coccyx*, but in the embryo it extends well beyond the rudimentary legs.

Darwin also drew attention to the vestigial structures which man carries, left-overs of his ancestral past: there is the vermiform appendix, which corresponds to a portion of the intestine of some herbivorous mammals. There are also in man the remnants of muscles found in animals and used to twitch the skin, or to turn and cock the ears—in fact some human beings can still use these muscles and can move their ears. Also the human fetus in the sixth month of pregnancy is covered with a coat of fine hair, called the languno, except on the palms of the hands and the soles of the feet, a reminder of the hairy coat of mammals.

Darwin focused on the hands as vital in man's struggle up the evolutionary scale, and deduced that the two-legged and ultimately erect position, which freed the hands to develop, must have happened early in man's history. As the hands became adept in using weapons and as man learned to use fire and to cook, less dependence was thrown on the teeth and jaws, which consequently reduced in size. Thus the prominent brow ridges which supported the strong muscles to work the jaws disappeared; and at the same time the skull top enlarged to accommodate the enlarged brain.

Darwin ascribed four factors as being fundamental to the development of man: natural selection, use and disuse, sexual selection and spontaneous variations. As for the mental and spiritual powers of man—those powers which Darwin's critics alleged most clearly differentiate man from the rest of the animals—he conceded that the difference between even the most highly organized ape and the "lowest savage" is vast.

But so, he pointed out, is the distance between that savage, "who has no word to express any number higher than four and who uses hardly any abstract terms," and the mind of a Newton or a Shakespeare. And he recalled vividly the Fuegians whom he had seen while on the voyage of the *Beagle* and who had then struck him as being much closer to wild animals than to civilized man, both in appearance and behavior.

Animal Talk

There is no fundamental difference, Darwin asserted, between the mental faculties of man and the higher animals. There is however a huge interval between the mental powers of one of the lowest fishes, say the lamprey, and one of the higher apes; yet this interval is filled with numberless gradations.

Pleasure, pain, happiness, fear and misery are emotions felt by the lower

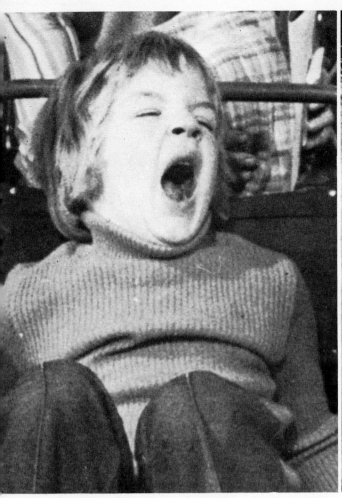

Darwin shocked the world with his proposition that pleasure and pain, happiness and sadness, fear and curiosity were emotions felt by higher animals as well as man. He showed how apes utter a sound like laughter when tickled under the arms (left) and that as a man yawns when bored or tired so do many animals (right). This, he said, was further evidence that man and apes had come from a common stock millions of years ago and that the difference between animals and man was one of degree not of kind.

animals as well as by man, and the physical effects of these emotions are similar. Fear makes the muscles tremble, increases the heart rate and respiration, erects the hair. Animals, as well as man, exhibit the maternal instinct, curiosity, memory, and the power to learn. The differences are those of degree, not of kind.

As for language, Darwin wrote: "The habitual use of articulate language is peculiar to man, but he uses in common with the lower animals inarticulate cries to express his meaning, aided by gestures and movements of the muscles of the face." Modern researches into the sonar language of dolphins would surely have strength-ened Darwin's arguments on the communication powers of the lower animals. So would anthropologists' observations on the structured social life of gorillas and wild dogs.

Darwin had hardly any fossil evidence of early forms of man to support his theories and he could therefore do little with any challenge to produce a "missing link." The first skull of a Neanderthal man, found in Germany in 1856, was thought to be an abnormal, pathological specimen; and similar doubts were expressed about Java man when he was found in 1889. Nevertheless, Darwin, that Sherlock Holmes of the scientific world, arrived by pure deduction at the conclusion that Africa was probably the cradle of mankind.

Missing Link

The evolutionary line of living things runs from the primordial cell, through the fish, the amphibians, the mammals, the New World and the Old World monkeys, and finally to man. Darwin believed that man's ancestors diverged from simian stock of the Old World, from extinct species allied to the gorilla and the chimpanzee. And because in each region existing species are closely related to extinct species of that same region, Darwin

thought it probable that remains of man's early ancestors would one day be found in Africa. The discoveries by the Leakeys in the Olduvai region in this century, even in this decade, have borne him out.

Similarly, in Darwin's time the principles of genetics and the basic laws of heredity had not yet emerged. Now we know, for instance, that human hemoglobin in its commonest forms differs at only three points from that of the gorilla, and that man has almost the same chromosome count as the apes.

Darwin, in a passage of self-analysis in his autobiography, wrote: "I have steadily endeavored to keep my mind free, so as to give up any hypothesis, however much beloved (and I cannot resist forming one on every subject), as soon as facts are shown to be opposed to it." And he attributed his success "to the love of science—an unbounded patience in long reflecting over any subject—industry in observing and collecting facts—and a fair share of invention as well as of common sense. With such moderate abilities as I possess, it is truly surprising that thus I should have influenced to a considerable extent the beliefs of scientific men on some important points."

227

COMPLAINTS

Zip Art

The nagging wife

Bitch!bitch!bitch!bitch!bitch!bitch!bitch!bitch!—all the world fears the nagging wife.

Everybody nags—even men. How many times have we had to endure—or been guilty of—continual harping on a subject, whether it is necessary or not—a mother constantly telling her adult children to wear warm underclothes or eat more, a wife continually exhorting her husband to stop drinking, cut down on his smoking or help more about the house.

From time to time we all feel strongly enough about loved ones risking health or not doing something we feel they ought to do. The fact that we go on about their shortcomings is sometimes described as "nagging." The "nagging wife," however, is an obsessive nagger, not a woman concerned about specifics.

For the obsessive nagger everything appears to be associated with pain. Her friends will let her down or do her a bad turn, her husband will be uncaring and ungrateful, her life will be harder than anyone else's, and she will be the agonized, brave little woman, innocent in the eyes of God but constantly put upon by mortals. We use the term "paranoia" to describe the general frame of mind we see here.

This type of paranoia is basically a feeling of persecution. We all know it in its mild form, the person who says things like "It always rains when I go on holiday." An exaggerated, and laughable, case of paranoia is that of the man who goes to a football game and, seeing the players form a huddle, thinks they are talking about him.

Have Bag Will Nag

The obsessive nagger's life will be organized around her paranoia so that the truth of her suffering will be plain to the world. She tends to be genteel but shabby: anything smarter would spoil the image of martyrdom. In her younger years she is often jilted, having unconsciously provoked the breaking up of a relationship in order to feed her paranoia. But she is destructive, too, and is likely sometimes to do the jilting herself because she is incapable of a normal form of loving.

In jobs she is a problem for both boss and workmates and will be a constant troublemaker for reasons totally invisible to others. If she is not fired, she quits only just in time to avoid it. Personnel managers are familiar with the type and would describe her as "having an unfortunate manner," or say there was a "personality clash." They are usually aware that there is nothing they can do about her except to try to smooth out the ruffled feathers of the others under her attack and hope that she will soon go and work for someone else.

As a shopper, she is the horror of all salesgirls and will complain about the goods, the service and the store until all others have lost the energy to cope with her. Although they might not necessarily understand the nature of her problem, all store managers recognize the type and have their own way of dealing with her. At one time a large department store began hiring out-of-work actors to pose as floor managers in order to give these women a butt for attack. The bogus floor manager would be castigated by his superior and fired. The satisfied customer would leave and the poor actor would sit back and wait for the next nagging customer, when he would get "fired" again. It went on and on.

The obsessive nagger is unleashing her mental and emotional problems onto other people, usually her husband, because he is the most convenient victim. How the husband reacts, of course, depends on his make-up and personality, but nagging women tend to marry rather pliable men who learn to live with the nagging the way they would live with toothache. They will often build up a resistance to the daily content of it so that it washes over them almost unnoticed, and yet they need the nagging as penance for some deep-rooted problem of their own. The sort of man who would lose his temper at being nagged is not likely to marry the nagging woman in the first place. Such a woman attracts to her a man whose own mental make-up is lacking some element of security, strength or self-possession, and her nagging fulfills a need for him whereas it would anger and frustrate a different type of man.

If the nagging is like continuous toothache to the husband, it is even worse for the nagging wife herself because the nagging is only the symptom of her basic problem, not the problem itself. Naggers are born, not made. The demanding child will become the nagging woman and she is a victim of fate as much as of her own emotions. She is living with eternal frustration and nags because of it, rather like a child cries because it wants to carry on playing without knowing that it is too tired to do so.

The nagging wife wants something very badly, but she does not know what and neither does anyone else. She therefore nags for or about everything that comes in sight, subconsciously hoping that the object, or the righting of a situation, will satisfy the gnawing need inside her. This unfulfilled desire is completely subconscious: she is no more aware of it than she is aware of what would assuage it—a never-ending search.

Basically, it stems from sexual repression. This is not be be confused with a lack of sexual activity or a lack of virility on the part of her husband. It goes much deeper than that. She has sado-masochistic tendencies due to the arrested development of her earliest emotional and sexual stages.

Chronic nagging is a disease. A constant level of nagging will be interrupted from time to time by a blazing row deliberately provoked by the nagging wife as a substitute for a normal sexual relationship.

Paranoia

Paranoia is the classic psychological condition, first categorized by Freud and caused by the deep-rooted guilt complex instilled in a baby by its mother. A small child, in its earliest stages of development, will begin to realize that, when it has defecated, it has produced something from its own body, it has created something. If the mother is appalled by this, by the need to clean her baby, then her attitude is transmitted to the baby and a guilt complex sets in. It is extremely harmful for a baby to be made to feel dirty and unloved because of a physical act which is part of its natural make-up. There are four things that all of us have to do from the day

we are born to the day we die—breathe, sleep, eat and defecate. Obviously, a person sent through life feeling that he or she ought not to be doing any one of those things is bound to have problems.

A normal child will go through several anal stages in its early existence. These are perfectly natural and pass in a normal succession pattern as the child advances. It will first realize it can and does defecate. It will then go on to playing with the feces, and pass through a stage of wanting sausages for breakfast, lunch and dinner before passing out of the simple anal stage towards the next stage. The nagging wife is suffering from sexual repression caused by arrested development at the early anal stage in her baby years. Because of the nature of the problem it is almost always passed on from generation to generation. This type of woman will instill guilt into her own children by treating them as though dirtying a diaper were a sin.

Bowel Trouble

She goes through life with a horror of bottoms, bowels and all anality. If she possibly can, she will hide or disguise the lavatory in her house and generally behave towards it the way the dragonlike village spinster behaves towards a licentious film or book. She overreacts to dirt .or to smutty jokes or to any form of sexual deviance, however slight.

All natural stages of development have a limited life, but the arrested development of one stage in a baby's life will affect the other normal stages. And so the sexual development of the child is affected by the anal horror, and a sado-masochistic tendency forms. The sexual tendencies will become very definitely anal instead of genital, thus perpetuating the guilt.

Although she will be shocked and angered by any allusion to unnatural intercourse, basically it is what she craves, although the attendant guilt would make it impossible for her to submit to it. She is destructive to normal sexual relations because she is not very interested in them. She will not get enough fulfillment from genital intercourse, especially performed in the normal position, and she will often use her nagging to provoke rows in order to avoid sex.

In normal people the intelligence is used to express love and affection, but the nagging wife will angle her intelligence towards provoking and carrying through arguments. She is

also very likely to get more sexual excitement and gratification from a sadistic row than from sexual intercourse with her husband. But, as we have already noted, her husband is likely to be the sort of man who needs her particular type of behavior and, while it is possible he could seek simple, straightforward sexual gratification outside the home, he probably finds some sort of fulfillment in her perverse actions.

Blue Pencil

The nagging wife is quite unaware of her repressed sexuality. It will not manifest itself as sexual desire: if it did, she would not nag. It is because the repression is so deep and so total that the outward symptoms of it appear to have nothing whatever to do with sexuality. She will get a certain amount of sexual gratification from seeing girlie magazines, especially the more pornographic variety, and the cycle of her needs is completed by making some act of rejection towards them. She will nag her husband if he reads them, or probably try to stop the local newsstand from even selling them.

The job ideally suited to her needs is that of censor (though she is not suited to the job). A local library censorship committee would give her the ideal outlet for her needs, desires, frustrations and problems. She would find tremendous sexual satisfaction in being able to read salacious passages from books and then ban them from the public. It is the problem of every censorship committee to keep this sort of person at bay although whether they ever manage to or not is debatable.

The typical nagging wife, however, once on such a committee, is not likely to be a militant member of it. She is not the type to take the floor in discussion or make any sort of exhibition of her presence. She will ease some of her frustration by merely being able to cast her vote towards banning something which she finds sexually titillating. This is the only way she can react with any form of pleasure to her gnawing feeling of guilt.

The life style and actions of the nagging wife become more understandable to the normal person when all these problems are taken into consideration. It no longer seems surprising that a person will be unable to react normally to other people when one understands that they are going through life feeling deeply guilty about the normal bodily functions. In

order to counteract her mother's early rejection, the nagging wife will vociferously reject all things she thinks of as "dirty" in order to feel that she is living up to the standard expected of her. Because her rejection and guilt are subconscious, she is unable to realize that the standard is false and unattainable.

The particular paranoid syndrome of the nagging wife is, in fact, becoming less common with the greater permissiveness of society and with the consequent relaxing of the attitudes of mothers. As society becomes more permissive, the opportunities for the individual to accustom herself to wider sexual freedom of both thought and action become greater. But the biggest step forward has been the willingness of mothers—even the ones emotionally crippled by their own mothers—to learn about the psychological, as well as the physical, needs of their babies.

But what about the obsessively nagging wife at large in society now? What do we do about her constant complaints and destructive actions? She can be helped by a psychiatrist, but a lifetime's problems cannot be cured overnight and she would have to have weekly consultations for at least five years for any sort of "cure" to take place. It is only after prolonged treatment under analysis that the paranoid nagger reaches an awareness of sexual repression, and that is just the beginning.

Willing Victim

From the point of view of the outsider, a little sympathy, whether false or genuine, would be gladly accepted because she has an inverse pride in the fact that her misfortunes are worse than anyone else's. Of course they are not, but do not try to tell her that. Beware, also, of giving her advice because, although she will ask for it, it will be disastrous. Her need is not for help, it is for the opportunity to watch something go wrong and then blame someone else for it. Her husband or friend should always make sure that the proposed solution to any problem comes from her first.

She is always happy to give advice although, as she makes such a mess of her own life, it would be unwise for anyone to take it, and she is the confidence trickster's dream if she happens to come into money. Her subconscious will push her towards losing it so that she can then sit back and wallow in the fact that her fears and suspicions were right and that she has, once again, been victimized.

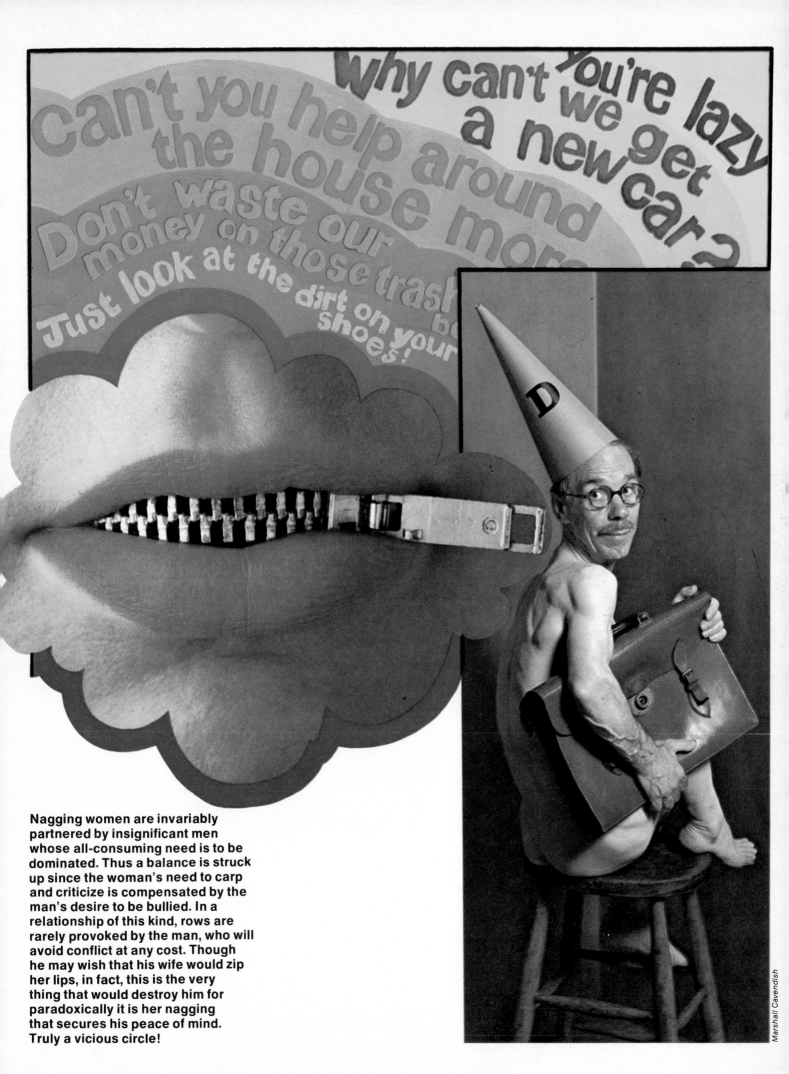

why can't you're lazy
we get
can't you help around a new car?
the house more
Don't waste our
money on those trash
Just look at the dirt on your
shoes!

Nagging women are invariably partnered by insignificant men whose all-consuming need is to be dominated. Thus a balance is struck up since the woman's need to carp and criticize is compensated by the man's desire to be bullied. In a relationship of this kind, rows are rarely provoked by the man, who will avoid conflict at any cost. Though he may wish that his wife would zip her lips, in fact, this is the very thing that would destroy him for paradoxically it is her nagging that secures his peace of mind. Truly a vicious circle!

Kim Sayer

Strange affairs

Sweet and sour meets bacon and egg. Will the marriage of opposites provide an exciting recipe for a happy and long-lasting relationship? Only time will tell . . .

Up until recently, most marriages have been bound by some pretty definite, if not stringent, conventions. But once marriage itself was so unconventional that little distinction existed between those married and those not. Sons born to a man's conventional wife had no advantage over his father's children by another woman. The term bastard was no slur, and usually just meant that a particularly grand person had honored your mother with his interest. In fact the bastard son of the founder of the Frankish Kingdom got a far larger share of his father's estate when he died than did the legitimate conventional sons.

The conventional aspects of marriage seem to have come about very gradually. Probably they were decided upon at an Anglo-Saxon synod (or convention of the church) that took place in the year A.D. 786. It took a

long while for the ideas of what was proper, normal and conventional in marriage to become established. Even in the tenth century it was usual to allow a seven-year trial marriage, and one year's trial marriage existed in Scotland until the Reformation, after which it became usual, as well as legal, for a marriage to last "till death us do part."

These early conventions underline the basic, widely accepted behavioral concepts of marriage. From the beginning marriage was a male orientated institution involving the protection of male sexual rights. The convention implied that the wife was her husband's property and so to seduce her was not so much a moral offense, but one far more serious in the eyes of man, an offense against property. And many of the unconventional aspects of marriage today

came about as a reaction to this presumption of ownership of women.

Whenever convention seeks to dictate behavior unconventionality will occur as a rebound phenomenon. And to see some of the reasons that lie behind the attractions of making socially unacceptable marriages today, it is only necessary to turn the pages of the history books back and examine the prohibitions that generated present-day unconventionality. This is seen particularly clearly with reference to the influence of the prohibitive marriage laws of the various churches.

For many years, with peoples the world over, there has been an anti-incest taboo and it is considered incestuous to marry a relative, especially a parent or a sibling. In the beginning, the early Christian church extended this prohibition to include

Camera Press

marriages of first cousins as well.

Later, however, the fathers of the church became so obsessed with incest phobia that they forbade even second and third cousin marriages. Eventually these prohibitions were extended to godfathers, godmothers, and at last even to relations of priests that had baptized, confirmed or married a person. On the other hand, at one time no Christian could marry a follower of any other religion, and for a Christian to marry a Jew involved the same penalty reserved for the

crime of bestiality. Remarriage was, of course, forbidden in the early Christian church—even if the first partner was dead.

Thus in the days of our forefathers, the various psychological bricks were laid down for the walls that still enclose many of our subconscious thoughts. The ancient definition of sin, the eating of the forbidden fruit, still holds good in man's subconscious today, and the persuasive delights of their sampling dictate the attitudes and behavior of modern

These four married couples have been re-paired in a way that may seem shocking to some people. But today mixed marriages are on the increase and problems of adjustment must be recognized and solved.

"liberated" men and women. Unconventional marriages often have an attraction on this score alone.

Although incestuous relationships that amount to a form of marriage infrequently come to light in modern society, researchers in this twilight

233

area of human liaisons have quite recently shown that "married life" between father and daughter is, in fact, quite common in remote country communities. This is so in many European countries and in both American continents.

By far the most interesting types of unconventional marriage, however, occur in a sexually less florid climate. Look at marriages in which one partner takes a mate from an ethnic group, or social class, that is so unusual as to be remarkable in everyday life. This is the classical "heiress-marries-truck driver" story, although the same phenomenon can be seen in some mixed marriages between very distinct racial groups.

A typical example was that of a Viscountess's daughter who married a plumber. The lady in question was a highly intelligent young woman, born of an aristocratic British family. She suffered from a reasonably common developmental abnormality in childhood, a bilateral cleft palate, complicated by a hare lip. This had been surgically repaired in an ex-

Widely differing intellectual capacities can cause problems in a true marriage of minds.

tremely skillful manner, but it left her with a "speaking through the nose" type of voice, which often follows such operations.

Although physically quite presentable, she grew up as the socially embarrassing "ugly duckling" in her family. As a teenager she felt the rejection of her social peers very strongly, decided to give up the easy life and became a nurse.

The Lady and the Tramp
While still in training she became pregnant by a young man who worked at the hospital as a plumber, and married him despite considerable family pressure to have an abortion and break up the relationship. This unconventional marriage has proved to be happy and continuing despite a wide social gap between the partners.

A less happy state of affairs occurs when a strong sense of the "forbidden" brings about a marriage. Many psychiatrists see this as an example of an unresolved Oedipus complex in action.

Oedipus will be remembered as having married, unwittingly, his mother and the Oedipus complex has been expanded to include the circumstance in which the natural love

between mother and son (or father and daughter) never matures into an adult situation. The son or daughter then remains in love with a "forbidden" love object, that is, father or mother.

As this is patently impossible in adult life, because it flies in the face of the sexual taboos of incest, there is a compulsion to form sexual liaisons with and in many cases to marry conventionally "forbidden" love objects. Only if a big "forbidden" label is attached to someone is it possible for a love affair to develop in such cases.

An attractive young white woman with a Roman Catholic religious background formed a series of sexual liaisons with colored men of various ethnic types. This caused much anxiety and parental opposition. Although the girl in question was upset by the attitude of her parents she seemed incapable of forming any relationship with a white consort.

Eventually after a number of quite serious sexual affairs with various colored men she married one. Three months later the couple were living apart but the woman in question still said she preferred colored men to whites.

Kim Sayer

Kim Sayer

A similar situation occurred in the case of the daughter of a successful stockbroker. At the age of 18 she ran away with, and married, a man who worked in a service station who could neither read nor write. The marriage lasted for 18 months. Within a year she had married a jazz musician who was also a drug addict. Again the marriage was short-lived. She is now engaged to an impecunious school-master with a flair for very left wing politics.

In both cases the young women had been brought up in good and loving families. The first girl had been the only girl, and father's favorite, in a family of four. In the other case there was a brother and another sister, but the father always made a special fuss of the young woman. She was the daughter of his first marriage and her own mother had died when she was a tiny child.

Both these women had a lasting, if largely unconscious, love affair of sorts with their fathers, which was never emotionally resolved. Their subsequent attraction for "forbidden men" is therefore psychologically

Mind your manners! Marriages rarely survive flouting class barriers and social conventions, however strong the bond of love.

quite explicable and similar behavior can be seen in other marriages that seem puzzling and unconventional.

Perhaps not so startling but never-theless evidence of similar psycho-logical needs, there are the marriages between elderly men and women young enough to be their daughters or granddaughters. These girls have not married men of their own generations because of an unconscious need to love a father figure. The men are usually marrying the only woman who ever really attracted them sexually—their own daughters. It is unfortunate that they are often referred to as "dirty old men."

Then there are sado-masochistic marriages, relationships of quite another nature. The root causes of the development of sadistic or masochistic tendencies in individuals are not entirely understood. One theory is that these inclinations develop in childhood.

Bizarre Tastes

It is difficult for an adult to perceive the degree of emotion that wells up in a child when he knows he is going to be punished or is being punished. Sometimes this emotional reaction can be so great that it overflows into the sexual sphere. A male child may have an erection when he is spanked or beaten. Repeated punishment like this soon creates a psychological reaction in which pain and sex are equated.

When the punished individual becomes excited sexually *only* by the infliction or the reception of pain, then a persistent sadistic or masochistic tendency can develop. In all probability the root causes of the development of a sadistic or a masochistic individual are the same in both sexes.

Now, although there are unconventional marriages based on sadistic or masochistic drives of an overt nature, in which the demand for a mate of a very rare and special type outweighs all the usual attractions or reasons for marrying "the girl next door," far more common is so-called psychic sadism or masochism.

This is demonstrated vividly in the case of the "lion" who marries the "lamb." A marriage of this sort often results in remarks like "I can't understand what she sees in him. He treats her like a slut or a beast. He's not her type at all."

Alternatively, there is the "worm that will never turn" type of man, whose unusual marriage demands are satisfied uniquely by the shrew and the chronic nagger. He is a man who desperately needs to be shrieked at, bullied, humiliated in public, belittled and abused. Only in this way is his psychic masochism satisfied.

Unconventional marriage, therefore, tells us something about one or other of the partners if the relevant behavior code can be cracked. Mary Brown, the typist, by all intents and purposes should have married Joe Green, the insurance man, but chooses Pedro Gonzales, the immigrant waiter, instead. This may simply mean that she prefers one over the other, but there could have been something about Pedro that made him so necessary as a healer, supporter or stimulator of Mary's crippled or distorted personality—something that explains the unconventionality of the union. Did the minister's son marry the call girl because he just happened to fall in love with her, or did her way of life appear to him a way out of an emotionally stifling existence that was impossible to resist? In many cases the skilled behaviorist can sort out some of these incredible situations that are usually so bizarre that they provide material for the novelist.

Do unconventional marriages work? Well, the marriage guidance counselors will tell you that very often they do, although failure rates are high compared with conventional marriages. The father-daughter type of marriage often seems particularly stable and satisfying.

The fact that we are living in a more mobile and in some ways less structured society will probably make unconventional marriages become rather more frequent, and this in time will make their unconventional nature seem less striking.

Unconventional marriages are commonplace in artistic circles. Shown here are director Roy Boulting and his young wife Hayley Mills, who as a child star spent her youth in adult company. Also shown is Pablo Picasso with Jacqueline Rocque, whom he finally married when he was in his eighties after they had been living together for over ten years. Picasso was renowned for his turbulent love-life.

Camera Press

236

Mechanical aptitude

Do you understand machinery, or does it baffle you completely? When your child asks, "What makes the car go?" do you say, "Gas," explain the principles of the internal combustion engine, or get off the hook by telling him to ask someone else? Men are generally supposed to understand machines and the physical workings of the world better than women and in most cases they do. On psychological tests of mechanical aptitude, men are usually superior. This could be, partly, because they have been encouraged from an early age to tinker with machinery; for while many little girls will play happily with a clockwork toy, a little boy will more often take it apart to see how it works.

If you love to repair machines, you already know that you have some sympathy with them, but many people could understand much better than they do the workings of everyday mechanics. Check the questions below to see how often you try to cope with mechanical problems or whether you just ignore them.

1. Your car refuses to start on a cold winter's morning. Do you
a. look under the hood?
b. telephone the garage?
c. leave it for a few minutes and try again?

2. Your dishwasher or washing-machine develops a noise like a soul in agony. Do you
a. call the repairman and then wash by hand?
b. adjust the water intake?
c. go on using it, but go into another room while it operates?

3. Your watch stops. Do you
a. shake it violently?
b. open it up?
c. take it back to the shop?

4. Your typewriter carriage jams. Do you
a. check that there is nothing on the desk, like a telephone directory, blocking its passage?
b. shout for help?
c. take off the front and examine it?

Your Approach

1. a. M **b.** H **c.** O
2. a. H **b.** M **c.** H
3. a. O **b.** M **c.** H
4. a. M **b.** H **c.** M

M=the Mechanical Approach, whether or not it is successful.
H=the Calling-for-Help Approach, even before you have tried to clear the trouble yourself.
O=the Ostrich Approach, the belief that, magically, the problem will go away without you or anyone else having to take action.

If you have at least one M score, then you may have more mechanical aptitude than you think; if you have none, are you really giving yourself a chance? Try the next set of questions to see if you have the basic orientation that you could develop.

Most of the problems require you to put yourself into the particular situation, to visualize what would happen if certain steps were taken. Psychologists call this knack visuo-spatial ability. How good is yours?

---

1. Compare the two pictures. Which room has the bigger echo?
2. In one minute, how many of the shapes on the right can you match up with the spaces on the far right?
3. Under 3a and 3b are three rudder positions. Which one is correct to steer each boat at sea to land?
4. Which do you think would weigh more, a golf ball or an empty cornflake box? Try picking them up.

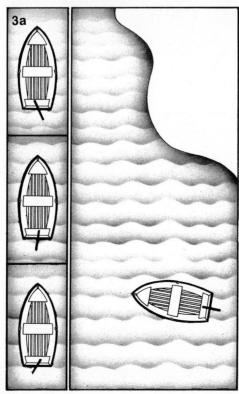

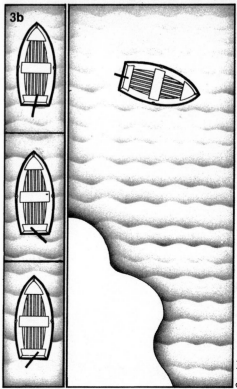

5. Do you save money by not switching on your car lights until the last possible moment?

6. What action would you take if there was no suction in your vacuum cleaner?

7. Which figures below can be made from the pattern on their right?

8. Can you explain how the contraption pictured below works?

How do you think you scored? This is not, of course, an exhaustive or standardized test, but it should give you some idea of whether you are right to call for help when faced with a mechanical problem!

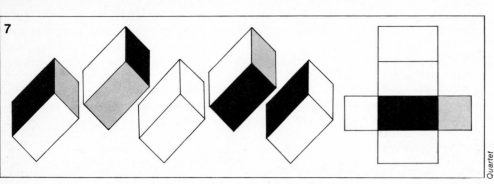

7

Quartet

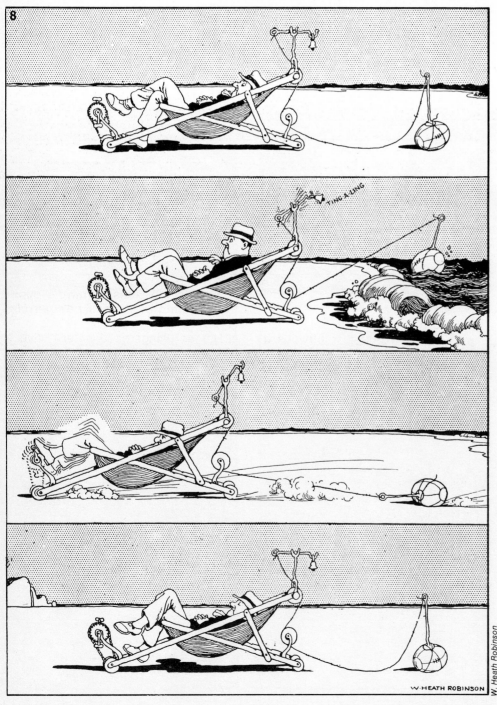

W. HEATH ROBINSON

W. Heath Robinson

Answers

1. The room on the top—it has no carpet or curtains to absorb sound.

2. All the shapes on the left can be inverted and turned to fit into the ones on the right.

A score of ten or more indicates good form perception, an important part of mechanical ability. This is one ability that seems to be innate and does not improve significantly with practice. Oddly, children often do better than adults on this sort of item.

3. For the boat on the left, the rudder should be turned so it is like the top picture. For the boat on the right, the middle picture is correct.

4. Both weigh about the same. If you pick up packets of identical weight, but unequal size, you find a curious illusion takes place—the smaller one will feel heavier.

5. No. A car generates its own electrical supply. Many intelligent adults do not understand electricity and indulge in magical thinking about it, though most of us are not quite so naive as Thurber's aunt, who thought that it leaked away unseen from any unplugged electrical point!

6. If the motor is working, the obvious thing to do is to look for a blockage; probably dust and human hair.

7. All the boxes are possible except for the one second from the left (as there is no long gray side on the flat piece).

8. No confirmed lazybones wants to be washed out to sea. This ingenious invention, ''The Safety Deck Chair for Giving Due Warning of the Approach of the Tide,'' works because the ball floats on the incoming waves, pulling a wire that rings a bell, which then stirs the sleeper into action. A few moments of quick pedaling will ensure another hour of peaceful sleep! The cartoonist, W. Heath Robinson, is associated with zany machines, gently satirizing the modern world. Many are more complicated and unworkable than this one. Are you so mechanically-minded? Maybe the right motivation could make you dream up something like this.

Your Mechanical Ability

7 or 8—you probably have the basic aptitude to solve most mechanical problems.

5 or 6—you are about average in mechanical ability.

0-4—your mechanical aptitude is not your strongest point.

238

Does it follow?

Logical thinking comes to us all as naturally as breathing. All our conversations and thoughts are either logical or nonlogical; either argumentative ("Travel is good for you"—making a point) or nonargumentative ("I like traveling"—just an observation). Aristotle, the Greek philosopher, defined man as "the reasoning animal." But if we can all reason, why do we differ so much? Emotions and wishes, of course, get mixed into our thinking, distorting judgment. And we all fall into the traps of false logic from time to time.

You can learn to recognize and avoid mistakes in your own thinking, and to deal with them in others' arguments. In real life, different people will come to different conclusions about the same facts. How would you have coped with the situation described by Mrs. Golda Meir, the former Israeli Prime Minister?

"Once in cabinet we had to deal with the fact that there had been an outbreak of assaults on women at night."

No one was in dispute of these facts. What should be done?

"One minister suggested a curfew: women should stay at home after dark."

Logical? Mrs. Meir did not think so.

"I said, 'But it is the men who are attacking the women. If there is to be a curfew, let the men stay at home, not the women!'"

Contrariwise Logic

Charles Dodgson was a lecturer in mathematics at Oxford University and a master of logical argument. He is better known as Lewis Carroll, whose brilliant books for children combined humor, inventiveness and a characteristic quirky logic that made them as popular with adults.

In *Alice's Adventures in Wonderland*, the Mad Hatter's unquestionable logic throws Alice into confusion when she is told to say what she means: "'I do,' Alice hastily replied; 'at least—at least I mean what I say—that's the same thing, you know.' 'Not the same thing a bit!' said the Hatter. 'Why, you might just as well say that "I see what I eat" is the same thing as "I eat what I see".'"

"Contrariwise," explains Tweedledee in *Through the Looking Glass*, "if it was so, it might be; and if it were so, it would be: but as it isn't, it ain't. That's logic."

Hidden Logic

"Bill must be doing well this year; he is taking his family to Europe for two months." Everyday statements like this follow a logical pattern of argument, called a syllogism. A syllogism has two premises and a conclusion:

Only people over 18 can vote. (first or basic premise)

You are not over 18. (second premise)

So you cannot vote. (conclusion)

Aristotle

The most famous syllogism of all time is Aristotle's:

All men are mortal.

Socrates is a man.

Therefore Socrates is mortal.

This seems elementary and obvious, a conclusion we do not need a formula to reach. Yet the syllogism was a breakthrough in thinking, and it affects us today.

Most of us, of course, do not set out our statements in such a precise fashion, but the underlying structure of our thinking often corresponds to this form. We frequently omit a premise, or even a conclusion. The missing basic premise in the statement about Bill would be something like "People who take their families to Europe for two months are doing well." By turning around the original statement we have a second premise ("Bill is taking his family to Europe for two months") and the conclusion ("Bill must be doing well this year.")

Many arguments sound more convincing in their incomplete state. "The police in England are unarmed and this works well. We should do the same in America." The missing premise is "Whatever works well in England will also work well in the United States"—an arguable point.

"I must get some skin cream like Mary's—she looks great these days." But will Mary's skin cream necessarily be good for you? (This also assumes that her radiance has anything at all to do with her cosmetics.) Arguments from false premises can be logically sound, in a technical way:

Elephants wear pink trousers.

Jumbo is an elephant.

Therefore Jumbo wears pink trousers.

Logical, but plainly untrue. To test any argument, both the basic premise and the steps following from it have to be examined.

False Logic

There are four possible combinations of premises and conclusion with respect to truth and falsity.

1. the premises may be true and the conclusion true

2. the premises may be true and the conclusion false

3. the premises may be false and the conclusion false

4. the premises may be false and the conclusion true

Can you pick out which types the following statements are?

a. Socialists are capitalists, and capitalists want to abolish private property, therefore Socialists want to abolish private property. (Type 4)

b. Cats climb trees; squirrels climb trees, therefore cats must be squirrels. (Type 2)

c. Human beings need water to live; I am a human being, therefore I would die without water. (Type 1)

d. Doctors are always right, so I never pay any attention to mine. (Type 3) This is absurd, of course. The false premise is followed by an inconsistent conclusion.

Examining isolated statements is not the same as taking part in a discussion or listening to people who try to convince us. Glaring errors are not always so easy to spot. There are many traps, or dirty tricks, that can be used. Learn to recognize and refute them.

Two Dirty Tricks of Argument: All or Some?

The most common form of dishonest argument is to say "A is B," when what is true is "Some A is B." This is

Mary Evans

239

the basis of prejudiced statements like "Women are illogical," "Blacks are lazy," "Redheads are quick-tempered." It would be technically possible to get at the truth of such statements, to discover if, for example, fat people do tend to be placid, but that would not be a basis for arguing about an individual case.

Statistical arguments tell us about tendencies or probabilities, not definite facts about individual people. In the same way, statistical information cannot be disproved by reference to individuals. When you come up against an argument where "all" is implied but only "some" is true, point out that this is so, and show that it is false.

Selected Cases

"My uncle Joe smoked 40 cigarettes a day and lived to be 98, therefore smoking cannot be harmful." Another dishonest trick. When evidence is statistical, one or two contrary instances do not disprove it.

Arguing from selected cases is, sadly, very common in matters of national importance. The case for capital punishment can point to a number of countries with no capital punishment and a large number of murders, and countries with capital punishment and a small number of murders; but this is not enough. Those opposed to capital punishment can select their evidence in the same way. Real proof would be an examination of the relationship of all four possible cases.

The way to tackle this kind of argument is not by dishonestly selecting your own opposing instances, but by pointing out the nature of the proof offered, and supplying or demanding the missing information. This of course often spoils a good rousing row!

CAPITAL PUNISHMENT FEW MURDERS	**NO CAPITAL PUNISHMENT FEW MURDERS**
CAPITAL PUNISHMENT MANY MURDERS	**NO CAPITAL PUNISHMENT MANY MURDERS**

Spot the Flaw

Examine the following arguments and see if you can test their validity. Try to pin down the kind of error shown.

1. Lee is an introvert so she would rather read a book than go to a party.

2. Mr. A. B. of Wisconsin writes, "Your vitamin plan has changed my life. I am more vigorous than I ever was 20 years ago." Think what our vitamin plan could do for you!

3. Politicians are corrupt; you cannot trust your Congressman.

4. The TV producer said, "No one has written to object to the program so I have no reason to think that everyone was not happy about it."

5. If you do not want to go to the concert you cannot be musical.

6. Speed limits on roads are useless. Far more accidents occur in urban areas where there are speed limits than in the rural ones with no speed limits.

7. When we first fished in this lake there were plenty of fish and we caught them easily. Now, so many have been caught that the rest are wise to us and keep away from the lines.

8. I know he is intelligent; after all, he is an independent voter.

9. If you're so smart, how come you're not rich?

10. I do not believe that contraceptive pills have any bad effects; I have always felt fine and so have my friends.

Answers

1. There is a hidden basic premise: "All introverts prefer books to parties." Lee is an introvert, therefore she prefers books to parties." If the first premise is right, the argument is correct.

2. There is a hidden second premise: "What is good for Mr. A. B. of Wisconsin is good for you." This is not necessarily true.

3. "All" is implied where "some" is true. The conclusion is not necessarily true.

4. The conclusion is not necessarily true.

5. The hidden basic premise, "Everyone who is musical wants to go to the concert," is untrue and the conclusion is not necessarily true either.

6. The premises are correct, but the conclusion, "Speed limits are useless," is incorrect. There are other factors involved.

7. Again, the premises are correct, but the conclusion is not necessarily true. There could be other reasons the fish are not biting.

8. The hidden basic premise, "All independent voters are intelligent," is not necessarily true.

9. There is another hidden basic premise. "All smart people are rich," is unfortunately not true.

10. This is an argument from selected cases which have no bearing on statistical evidence. Because several people have no bad effects does not mean that this is true for the great majority.